The Majlis:
A Meeting Place

Abbey of San Giorgio Maggiore

17th International
Architecture Exhibition
La Biennale di Venezia

Caravane Earth
2021

TABLE OF CONTENTS

Introducing The Majlis

The word "majlis" مجلس stands for a place to receive guests. It is also a word for assembly. It is a structure that embodies the bridge between the personal and the public. It is a space of hospitality that preserves tradition and nurtures the emergence of new communality.

The Majlis is a multi-layered nomadic project created for the 17th Venice Biennale of Architecture. It comprises an architectural object, an exhibition, and a garden, all three hosted by the Abbazia di San Giorgio Maggiore. At its core is a bamboo structure with tent panels made of pure wool. The Majlis is a ground for communication, cohabitation, and collaboration. It is an ongoing experiment in the actual practice of living and working together. It invites a vast array of possible answers to the main question of the Biennale: "How will we live together?"

The Majlis is the inaugural project of Caravane Earth, a foundation based in the Netherlands with a mission to seed, practise, and promote ethical entrepreneurship and well-being through art, craft, architecture, agriculture, and education. We work towards positive systemic impact in social, cultural, and ecological realms. Caravane Earth supports craftspeople and strives to preserve distinct material cultures around the world, introduces organic agriculture in extreme climatic conditions of West Asia and North Africa, enhances connectedness of the region, and enables its participation in numerous intercultural dialogues.

This book is meant to be more than simply a catalogue about the Majlis. Here, we are presenting research conducted by Caravane Earth during the last three years and the key ideas that form our philosophy and agenda. It will highlight the main elements of the Majlis project and give both an introduction to members from our community of experts and a history of the phenomena that Caravane Earth has encountered during its research.

The following chapters are organised according to key elements of the Majlis: Exhibition, Architecture, Craft, and Earth. In the first chapter, Thierry Morel, the curator of the Majlis exhibition, introduces us to its history, themes, and rationale; we interview members of the Sheikh Faisal Bin Qassim Al Thani Museum about the workings of their institution; researcher Nailya Golman gives insight into a selection of artefacts from the Majlis Exhibition; Dr Sarah Johnson of the Dutch National Museum of World Cultures provides historical context for khayamiya carpets; Irini Gonou discusses her contribution in the form of the Majlis Banner; Caravane Earth's resident photographer Jörg Gruber reflects on the process of documenting the labour that went into the project's creation; and Alaloui Ouajid Moulay Said explains some of the essential aspects of the curation of Islamic art and the importance of traditional architecture.

In Architecture, we present a broad variety of perspectives and experiences in the field. Simón Vélez and Stefana Simic, the architectural duo behind the bamboo framework of the Majlis, tell the story of their connection to both the material and the resulting structure; we chronicle the history of Caravane's foundational research, the Art Village; we feature exclusive material from the archive of the master architect Abdel Wahed El-Wakil; and we interview Harriet Wennberg, Executive Director at The International Network for Traditional Building, Architecture & Urbanism (INTBAU) about the approach of the organisation.

The Craft section establishes Caravane's deep commitment to the world of craft, its practitioners, supporters, and the issues surrounding its further development and preservation. We chronicle the work of the Moroccan weavers who created the wool tent panels and speak with the Colombian workers responsible for cultivating the bamboo for the Majlis; Nina Mohammad-Galbert takes us through her work as the Creative Director at the Artisan Project; we interview David Linley, the Earl of Snowdon, on his particular relationship and approach to craft; and we hear from Marjorie Hunt, a folklife curator and education specialist with the Smithsonian, about the institution's work to support crafts and craftspeople.

Finally the closing section, Earth, features conversation about the literal and metaphorical foundation for both the Majlis and Caravane Earth. Todd Longstaffe-Gowan takes us on a walk through the Majlis Garden and we provide some facts and figures about the unique varieties of plants therein; we introduce one of the cornerstone projects of Caravane Earth, Heenat Salma Farm, detailing some of the critical work being done there and providing an introduction to the agricultural practice of Filāḥa; Nana Oforiatta Ayim narrates her experiences running the ANO Institute of Arts and Knowledge; and Tim Ingold, Chair of Social Anthropology at the University of Aberdeen, delivers an essay on the origins of the word "human" and the affinity of humans with soil.

Fahad Al-Attiyah: the Majlis and the Biennale's Main Question

Fahad bin Mohammed Al-Attiyah is the managing director of Caravane Earth. Here, he gives an introduction to both Caravane Earth and the Majlis, and discusses the ways in which the project relates to the main question of the 2021 Venice Architecture Biennale: "How will we live together?"

Caravane Earth was established precisely to consider how we all live, to draw attention to the importance of art, craft, architecture, agriculture, and education, and to work towards making real, significant change.

We believe these goals are very much in line with the overall theme of the 2021 Venice Biennale. We recognise that we all need to eat, and therefore there is an agricultural aspect to the foundation. We understand that we all need shelter, so there is an architectural aspect to our work. We realise we all need to have warmth, and thus we have a textile division and are focused on the wearable aspect of these materials. Finally, we also know that we are creatures who are creative in nature, and therefore there is always a creative aspect to our work that complements these other needs.

The Majlis is our inaugural project and it gives us the chance to present the foundation's research and programme at the Venice Architecture Biennale. The main purpose of The Majlis is to illustrate the importance of intercultural dialogue and mutual education, to demonstrate the power of traditional knowledge and techniques in dealing with the major planetary issues of the present.

The central architectural structure that we have built in Venice is the product of an international collaboration between craftspeople from Colombia, Morocco, and Italy. It is a study on natural materials, on preserving and reconstructing traditional knowledge in different localities around the world. We aim to reintroduce ancient principles that have proved themselves through the centuries to be resilient and to serve the people within any habitation. The bamboo we are using for the core of the structure was harvested, measured, and prepared for transportation by farmers and carpenters from Manizales, the central region of Colombia. The textiles for the Majlis were made in Morocco from pure local wool and then woven together in different locations across the country. In Venice, these elements are being carefully assembled by local craftspeople through dialogue with the material's producers.

The word "caravane" is used to describe a group of people on the move from place to place. This is in fact the future of the Majlis, which after the Biennale will continue on its journey from Venice, while the beautiful garden at the Abbazia di San Giorgio Maggiore will remain. The Majlis will reach many parts of the world to spread its message, beginning with the Qatar National Museum in the year 2022.

The Caravane Earth's Majlis is not just an exhibition. While it showcases great architectural expertise and symbolises the values of craftsmanship, tradition, and community (all close to Caravane Earth's values), the Majlis will also provide a spectacular platform for reflecting on our collective future on planet Earth. International experts from many different fields will share this platform to discuss how we will live together in a world of rapid change.

L'Abbazia
di San Giorgio
Maggiore

The Majlis: A Meeting Place   Introduction

The Benedictine Abbazia di San Giorgio Maggiore is located on the island of the same name in the Venetian lagoon. There is documentary evidence of a church existing on the site in the 8th century, while the abbey was founded in the 10th century; the original buildings, however, were destroyed by an earthquake in 1223.

In the 1560s, during the Venetian Republic, Andrea Palladio began to rebuild the monastery. The refectory was finished first, for which Paolo Veronese was commissioned to paint the *Marriage at Cana*, measuring almost seven by ten metres. The Benedictines liked the architect's work and Palladio was asked to continue working on the building. In 1565 he prepared a project for a new church and a second cloister. The model he proposed was quickly approved and a year later construction began. Although most of the work was completed during Palladio's lifetime, the main staircase, the new facade of the monastery, the novitiate, the infirmary, and the guesthouse were completed after his death – by 1610.

The Venetian Republic lost its independence in 1797. It was occupied first by French troops, then came under Austria's control, and eventually became part of the Kingdom of Italy, which at the time was dependent on Napoleon Bonaparte's France. The fall of the republic resulted in the loss of many masterpieces from the abbey's collection. After the abbey closed in 1806, it was turned into an arms depot and barracks, and served as a military garrison for the next hundred years. The church, however, remained active after the abbey's closure, with Mass still celebrated there, but without a community of monks.

The revival of the Benedictine community began in 1951. The church was given in concession by Count Vittorio Cini and restored. Monks from the Praglia community began to settle there, and in 2012 the monastery finally became part of the Abbazia di Praglia. Now the abbey is not only a functioning monastery and an architectural monument, but also an exhibition space for contemporary art and for masterpieces of Italian painting that survived the Napoleonic Wars.

The Majlis: A Meeting Place   Introduction

The Majlis: A Meeting Place   Introduction

Padre Noberto Villa of the Abbazia of San Giorgio Maggiore

Dom Noberto Villa is the Abate Emeritus of the Abbazia of San Giorgio Maggiore. He spoke with Thierry Morel about the theme of the Biennale, the connections between the abbey and the Majlis, and the relevance of craft in a spiritual context.

THIERRY
MOREL:

How do you feel the Majlis reflects on the primary questions of the Biennale (how will we live together?) and what role does the abbey play in this process?

PADRE
NOBERTO VILLA:

The Majlis reflects on the fundamental answers to this question, because the Majlis is the soul of the life of a village, of a community; at the centre of the village is this meeting tent that favours the virtuous interweaving of human and social relations, representing a profound aspect to this question. It is fundamental to rediscover the spiritual and cultural roots that delineate our human cohabitation, in order to live together. I think that the very fact that the Majlis is placed in the cloister of a Benedictine abbey – in the glorious abbey of San Giorgio Maggiore, with its 1,000 years of history – adds value to the cultural and spiritual aspect of the place. Thanks to the Majlis a dialogue is created in this place, the house of God. Placing the Majlis here, in the monastery, following the tradition of spirituality, of the Benedictine culture of hospitality and dialogue, creates a virtuous resonance, which highlights and underlines the cultural and spiritual roots of the Majlis – as a meeting place and an expression of a culture and spirituality that has crossed the centuries to reach us, and that today can be measured against our present-day realities.

T: Could you reflect on the history of both Venice, and more specifically San Giorgio, as intercultural meeting places between the East and West?

N: I think that the reality of Venice, in its historic, cultural, and spiritual dimension, is one that is unique in its values and in how it has expressed itself over the centuries. It is a profoundly spiritual reality that has elevated all forms of human expression; a cultural spirituality. Contemplating Venice, you see that it is a universe unto itself, made of sky, land, and sea. It is like a gem set in this particular universe of the lagoon. This reality has allowed Venetian civilisation to maintain a certain autonomy, one that favoured the various ways of expression that this city state developed. This is a city where the cultural, spiritual, and social dimension has assumed a whole range of particular expressions, precisely because of the special characteristics of this universe, of the Serenissima, that marked all its actions, be they political, economic, social, or cultural; all its actions were marked by this particularity. These interactions of Venice can be seen in its contacts with China, with the Near East, and through these relations one can see how Venice absorbed and integrated elements of other cultures. It can be described as a constant search for an answer to the questions posed by life. This dynamic approach, which created such fertile ground, traversed the centuries of its millenary history. You can see this permanence of the fabric of the city in its skyline of towers, steeples, and domes. So, it can be described as a deep soul, whose main fruit is its expansive human element. The choice to set up and relaunch the expression of the Majlis in this Biennale is particularly significant in that it happens in the context of a Benedictine abbey. It is a dialogue between the Majlis, an expression of caravan cultures and the desert, and a Benedictine abbey. I believe that as a result a virtuosic dialogue has been created: the Majlis is the symbol and the soul of a culture and spirituality that has crossed centuries. This is the soul of this historic journey. A Benedictine abbey represents a life-space that Saint Benedict placed under the keyword of peace. The key point of Benedictine spirituality is peace. Peace as a gift from God and as man's response to God as to how to fully embrace what Saint Benedict's view on our main mission is: to desire life and see happy days. These two elements are key to the spirituality and rule of Saint Benedict. Here we are on the fertile ground of life, the welcoming of life, of dialogue, of hospitality. This meeting and merging of profound spirituality with the realities of life: this, I believe, unites the Benedictine experience and the symbolic experience of the Majlis.

T: What can you say about the garden and the relationship with nature?

N: In my view, placing the tent here in the cloister, in this Eden-like space, in all its beauty, all this is enhanced by the art works in the gallery-space that remind one of the cultural and spiritual legacy of the Majlis. It is interesting to note that the interior part of the exhibition represents cultural depth, and the soul of the Majlis is represented physically outside, in the garden. The space of life has always been interpreted as a

search to recreate the harmony of Eden, of creation. The fact that the Majlis is presented to us in this bounty of nature is very significant and fully in line with the views and thoughts of the monastery. It is essential to interpret this as a quest for spirituality, because this spirituality is the keystone that helps explain the meaning of life, a true spirituality that must be answered to.

T: Finally, various examples of artisanal work can be seen throughout the exhibition and the monastery – what would you say is the significance of craft in a spiritual context?

N: Saint Benedict recognises the role of artisans in his rule, because everything must act in the function of the promotion of life, of the good in life. This applies to all dimensions. Artisanship has characterised the life of monasteries since the very beginning: from illuminated manuscripts, sculpture, columns, frescos, mosaics, fisheries, bee-keeping – an infinitely varied richness, an echo of continuous creation, which is life. Artisanship is participating in the act of creation, reflecting on it and on the human element involved. Therefore the Church, the Majlis, the house, and the palace are all different expressions of the same.

Exhibition

The Majlis is a result of practical research into how we can synchronise our intentions, efforts, policies, and practices to live together in peace with one another and with nature. The exhibition contextualises the Majlis, featuring the people and materials involved in its construction. Showcasing artworks and rare artefacts from the Sheikh Faisal Bin Qassim Al Thani Museum in Qatar, the Dutch National Museum of World Cultures in the Netherlands, the Scuola Grande di San Rocco of Venice, the monastery of San Lazzaro degli Armeni in the Venetian lagoon, and private collections, the project presents a platform for transnational, transcultural, and transhistorical exchange.

The concluding part of the Majlis exhibition is a film and a series of photographs by Jörg Gruber that document the different forms of labour that were involved in realising the project: the surviving practices of herding, shearing, dyeing with natural pigment, and weaving on traditional looms in Morocco, as well as the processes of selecting bamboo and putting together the resilient construction in Colombia. The artisans, their tools, and materials themselves narrate the story of the Majlis – a story that may offer a key to our main question: how will we live together?

The Majlis: Curatorial Narrative

Dr Thierry Morel is a curator, critic and art historian. He has worked on projects ranging from exhibitions, books, film, television and museum collaborations across the world. As the curator of the Majlis Exhibition, here he provides an explanation of its contents, themes, and conception.

The majlis, a traditional meeting place in Arab culture, is a symbol of hospitality, exchange of ideas, and transmission of oral heritage and music for nomadic people.

Three years ago, with a view to creating a winter art and craft residency in the desert of Qatar, Caravane Earth commissioned the Colombian architect Simón Vélez, one of the foremost pioneers of the use of bamboo, with fellow architect Stefana Simic, to design a contemporary interpretation of a majlis, using the resources of talented artisans from Colombia to Morocco. In spite of delays to this beautiful and idealistic project caused by the Covid pandemic, in the end the structural elements of the Majlis were produced.

The theme of the 17th International Architecture Exhibition in Venice, proposed by its curator, architect Hashim Sarkis, is "How will we live together?" This vital question inspired Caravane Earth to put forward an application for the Venice Biennale, with the Majlis as its centrepiece.

The seclusion, peace, and spirituality of the Abbazia of San Giorgio Maggiore presented itself as the most suitable environment for the Majlis. The very fact that it was still inhabited by a small community of Benedictine monks also played a part in this choice. Since the 10th century, the island of San Giorgio has been an example of how a community could live together in harmony with itself, with the world at large, and with nature. The idea of the Majlis appealed to the monks as well as to Claustra Onlus, the representative of their artistic foundation, and they agreed to host it in the garden of the Abbazia.

I felt also that the Majlis should be set in a garden that would welcome and surprise the visitors. The idea was that it should reflect two aspects. The first is the ancient tradition of monastic gardens that provided food and medicine for the monks, as well as allowed them to study botany. Secondly, the garden should evoke the fact that Venice was a major intersection at which most plants from the East were introduced to the rest of Europe. The Benedictine monks already had a few hens, a cockerel, and several tortoises, and a new home was built for them out of bamboo and wool left over from the Majlis. The vegetable garden was also enlarged with a greater variety of vegetables, fruits, and aromatic and medicinal plants. We invited Todd Longstaffe-Gowan, a landscape architect and leading specialist in the history of European gardens, to work on the project.

Realising, however, that both the word "majlis" and its meaning were unfamiliar to many people outside of West Asia and North Africa, we decided to illuminate and contextualise the concept and the culture around it with an exhibition of carefully selected artefacts related to the majlis, ranging from textiles and carpets to decorative panels, ceramics, glass, leather items, Quran manuscripts, and various objects of traditional nomadic life.

The exhibition also includes musical instruments traditionally played in the majlis. Although the Islamic tradition favoured religious musical expression as an adornment of religious texts, in practice, non-liturgical or secular music was frequently played in the majlis to accompany chanting, poetry, and tales.

The role played by Venice in the Majlis exhibition goes beyond that of a host city. For centuries Venice has been the meeting point between East and West. Venice imported and stocked precious spices, textiles, ceramics, and other goods from distant ports in the eastern Mediterranean. Through this process Venetians acquired a variety of ideas from Byzantine and Islamic cultures. These buoyant commercial exchanges were the source of Venice's wealth and unique atmosphere.

Venetian merchants notably traded with Turkey, Egypt, Syria, and Palestine, as well as with Persia and the countries of the Silk Route. They gained insight into Islamic culture through personal contact with Muslim trading partners. The architecture and decoration of the Basilica of San Marco and the Palazzo Ducale most visibly reflect the impact of Byzantine and Islamic imagery.

Textiles, carpets, and other objects selected for the exhibition are expressions of these fruitful exchanges. They include the celebrated San Rocco Mamluk carpet, created in Egypt and yet kept in Venice for almost five hundred years in the Scuola di San Rocco; and ceramics like the rare Kütahya pieces from the Monastery of San Lazzaro Degli Armeni. Yet the scope of artistic influences is so intricate and intertwined that it is sometimes impossible to establish the exact origin of a decorative pattern and the specific market for an artefact. Venetian artisans, notably those working with glass and textile, embraced these Eastern influences and in turn created their own artefacts that were successfully exported throughout the trading routes of Venice.

The exhibition aims to capture the essence of these cultural exchanges, while employing ethically sourced sustainable materials and traditional craftsmanship.

The film and photographs presented in the exhibition are the work of cinematographer Jörg Gruber, and they document with great poetry the commitment, skill, and love that craftswomen and craftsmen from Colombia and Morocco invested in the creation of all the parts of the Majlis construction. One of the most interesting aspects of this project was to travel to Morocco with the architects and Prerna Saraff, guided by Nina Mohammad-Galbert, to discover the wool markets in the Atlas Mountains, and to meet the very artisans that were to produce all the textiles destined to protect and adorn the Majlis. Their dedication, skills, and passion for their work were truly awe-inspiring. Jörg took their portraits and captured the processes of their work such as herding, shearing, dyeing with natural pigments, and weaving on traditional looms, as well as the processes of selecting, chopping, slicing, and assembling the bamboo. In the end, the bamboo structure, handcrafted in Colombia and assembled in Venice, and the Moroccan textile roof panels and carpets that cover and adorn it, come together as the architectural embodiment of Caravane Earth's mission and values, and a testament to the Biennale's theme of living together. The contributing artisans see their work complemented by the expertise of their fellow craftspeople. It is a project that creates a beautiful dialogue between their personalities and skills.

The exhibition, held in the vaulted galleries of the Abbazia, is therefore meant as a journey through the origin and meaning of the majlis towards its contemporary interpretation. This reinterpretation is intended as a homage to traditional crafts that are still vibrant in so many communities around the world.

The Majlis construction appears as a surprise at the end of this route. It is set in a luxuriant and colourful garden filled with borders of flowers, bushes, fruits, vegetables, and medicinal and fragrant plants, intricately organised in rows resembling the geometric patterns of the San Rocco Mamluk carpet. Not unlike this extraordinary carpet, the Majlis garden forms a symbolic cosmography of a small, earthly paradise.

The installation and the exhibition not only make use of traditional arts and crafts from different regions of the world, they demonstrate how craftsmanship, combined with respect for nature, are even more relevant today, in a world struggling with climate change and loss of traditional cultures.

The Majlis in San Giorgio showcases an architecture in harmony with its surrounding natural world. Craftsmanship is not just a practical discipline; it is also a process of education, a way of life, and a gift to future generations.

In conclusion, The Majlis: a Meeting Place is a work of international craftsmanship, architecture, and design – a fusion of work from Africa and Latin America steeped in the tradition and spirit of nomadism. Whether the nomadic way of life and its values are threatened in the modern world is a question worth posing, and answering.

The life of this project started on the drawing board, continued in the artisans' workshops, and finally comes to fruition as the Majlis hosts discussions and symposia organised by Caravane Earth, with our many collaborators including the Smithsonian Institution, INTBAU and UNESCO. Together it provides some important answers to the question posed by the Biennale: "How will we live together?"

Artefacts from the Majlis Exhibition

Researcher Nailya Golman contextualises highlights from the Majlis exhibition, providing insight and background for a selection of diverse artefacts. These stories and cultural contexts allow us to glimpse the important histories these objects can reveal.

Egypt, *c.* 15th–16th century
Scuola Grande di San Rocco

The Majlis: A Meeting Place

The San Rocco Mamluk carpet

At nearly ten metres long, this carpet is possibly the largest of its kind in the world, and ranks among the most powerful testimonies of the commercial, cultural, and artistic exchanges between Venice and the Orient that flourished during the 16th century.

A document dating from 1568 and preserved in the Scuola di San Rocco records that the "tapedo grando caierin" (large Cairene carpet) was in the confraternity's collection by this time. It is unknown how and when it was acquired, though it has been suggested that its acquisition may be linked with a decision taken by the confraternity in 1541 to purchase a pair of carpets as ornaments for the church, with a view to dressing the Scuola's altars when ambassadors or other dignitaries visited. The importance of the "tapedo" is underscored by the fact that its care has traditionally been entrusted to the Scuola's Guardian Grando pro tempore.

The San Rocco carpet was produced in Cairo, a leading centre of carpet weaving from the late 15th to the mid-16th century. Its design is similar to late Mamluk style carpets, which are characterised by a central medallion surrounded by smaller geometric motifs forming a kaleidoscopic appearance.

The complexity and refinement of the decoration of the San Rocco carpet, woven in three colours – red, blue, and green, with no white highlights nor dark brown outlines – and its three octagonal representations of the cosmos, separated by a thin perpendicular framing along the longer sides, is similar to the Blumenthal carpet in the Metropolitan Museum in New York.

The San Rocco carpet was for many years consigned to the Scuola's storerooms. It was rediscovered in 1986, and now ranks among its most treasured possessions. There are fewer than ten such carpets in existence, and of these the San Rocco Mamluk is the most distinguished and best preserved.

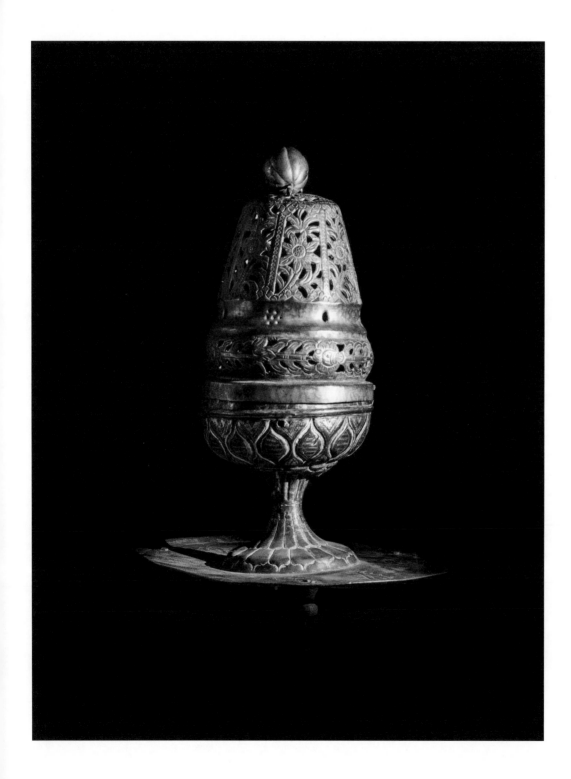

The Majlis: A Meeting Place Exhibition

Incense Burner

When one is in Qatar, one can frequently sense pleasant, sweet, and woody notes in the air. The source of the aroma is usually a delicate object shimmering with colourful decorations from which a trickle of smoke rises. This is how you burn bakhoor – a traditional wood-based incense that is more popular in the Arab world than the incense sticks that are customary in India and South-East Asia. Censers with bakhoor – called mabkhara – can be found everywhere: its smoke is used to infuse clothes with scent; it is used to welcome guests into majlises as well as mosques. It is thought that bakhoor brings calm and helps with concentration. The precise composition of aromatic oils differs from one producer to another, but the traditional basis of bakhoor remains the same – oud, the oily heartwood of lign-aloes. A household mabkhara, encountered inside the homes of practically every country in the Arab world, has several slightly different forms. One of the traditional variants, stored in the National Museum of Qatar, has the shape of a vertical tower with a rectangular base and a thinner middle part, with relief designs along the perimeter and four angular protrusions facing upwards. Between them, a metal bowl is placed, nested inside the tower – the incense is placed inside to smoulder on some coals, protected by the walls from gusts of wind. Traditionally, such a mabkhara was made from soft stone, wood, or clay, and decorated with hammered designs, cuttings, mirrors, or glass. The most common mabkharas on sale today are made of metal or glass; the heating element in many of them is electric, powered from a socket.

Iran, 1880s
FBQ. 7403 / Sheikh Faisal Bin Qassim Al Thani Museum

The Majlis Carpet

Today the word "majlis" is usually used to refer to official gatherings, various government bodies, or a specific format for receiving guests. But traditionally a majlis is also a physical space, a reception room, or a place for discussion, or even a separate tent in case of nomads. In the everyday sense, it is a transition zone from private life to public, where everything that takes place is organised according to the rules of hospitality. This Iranian majlis carpet from the late 19th century is a large piece of fabric made from sheep and camel wool. Such carpets were made to fully cover the floor during general meetings, and only a few have survived to this day in their original state. Thanks to the large geometric patterns on these carpets, merchants often cut them into several parts, following the contours of the pattern segments, and then sold the resulting pieces separately. The pattern, however, had its own meaning: it literally sketched out a map for all of the meeting's participants, showing the traditional scenario of events. The hosts, along with an imam, were meant to sit at one side, as if "at the head" of the carpet, while around them at the edges there was room for guests. Coffee tables, dishes with food, and boards for games – chess, for instance – stood at the centre. The gathering could involve the performance of a hakawati – a traditional Arabic storyteller – both instead of an imam or alongside him.

Kütahya, Turkey, 18th century
Congregazione Armena Mechitarista, Monastero Armeno
Mechitarista di San Lazzaro degli Armeni, Venezia

Oil Lamp Element

This fragment of an oil lamp, shaped like a ceramic sphere and featuring a band with a floral ornament and a pattern with roundels in blue glaze, is a ceramic specimen made in Kütahya in the 18th century. It continues the traditions of Iznik cobalt painting, used to decorate white ceramics and porcelain. The technique was most probably borrowed from Iran by the craftsmen of Iznik. A fashion for household objects made with white porcelain and ceramic and decorated with blue painted motifs emerged in the 14th and 15th centuries, thanks to Middle-Eastern masters who adopted the Chinese Yuan dynasty tradition of cobalt painting. A similar manner of painting became one of the foremost styles in the Iznik ceramics school, but its ornamental component underwent important changes, and specimens from the classical period of the golden age of Iznik ceramics (15–17th centuries) differed vastly from their Asian counterparts when it came to pattern. This period is widely considered to be the international golden age of Ottoman ceramics: around the middle of the 16th century the craftsmen of Iznik, producing tiles, tableware, and decorative objects, had their own colour palette and a style that was recognisable throughout the world. In the 18th century the sun set on Iznik, and the centre of ceramic production moved to Kütahya, where hereditary potters were mainly of Armenian descent. Ceramics from this school often feature Cyrillic monograms, Armenian script, and Orthodox saints, although Islamic motifs are also present: tiles from this school were also used to decorate mosques. The traditional ornaments of Syria, India, and Iran became a major source of inspiration, both because the Armenian diaspora in Turkey had well-established trade connections with these countries, and the fashion for Turkish art was gaining popularity in Europe. The work of ceramicists from Kütahya, located between Europe and Asia, developed rapidly and successfully – it was here that the trade routes intersected, which allowed local craftsmen to pick up on fashion trends and supplement their own techniques.

Ushak "Lotto" Carpet

This antique carpet, created in the knotted-pile technique, was made at the beginning of the 17th century in Anatolia, using techniques that were invented and gradually developed in the 16th and 17th centuries, and is where most of the classical examples of such carpets come from. This particular carpet is remarkable due to its bright colours and a characteristic pattern of complex arabesques with flowers made out of triangular shapes, inscribed into golden squares and surrounded by a pattern. The border of the carpet is decorated with an intricate ornament resembling the so-called pseudo-Kufic decoration or Kufesque, i.e. ornamental decorations imitating the Kufic script – a kind of Arabic script. It was used for copying important texts, primarily the Quran, from the end of the 8th century to the beginning of the 11th century. It was also used in architectural structures and objects, where Quran quotations written in this script underscored the sacred character of the object or structure. With time, this somewhat grandiose form of writing became an illegible decorative element. Objects with pseudo-Kufic ornaments were in high demand in the West as bearing the imprint of the high culture of the Islamic world. Carpets in paintings by Hans Holbein the Younger or Lorenzo Lotto (these artists were not the only ones to portray such carpets, but several types of carpet were named after them – for example, this "Lotto" carpet)

are a testament to this demand, along with the way in which many European artists used Kufesque to decorate the clothes of Biblical characters, especially when portraying events taking place in the Holy Land. It is thought that during the Crusades, Europeans considered Kufic script to have been written during the time of the Old and New Testaments. In the late Middle Ages Islamic culture was taken to be highly developed and sophisticated, so the Western consumer, unable to read Arabic, associated the Kufic script and pseudo-Kufic ornament, which were indistinguishable to them, with wealth, mysticism, science, and other hallmarks of the generalised image of the East.

Spain, 17th century
FBQ. 263 / Sheikh Faisal Bin Qassim Al Thani Museum

Glass Oil Lamp

Glass oil lamps such as this were used in the Islamic world to light up the interiors of communal buildings, such as mosques or medreses. Lined up in rows, these fragile vessels were hung down from the ceiling using long chains, inserted through eyelets which stood out along the glass circumference. Such lamps were traditionally decorated by Quranic inscriptions taken from the 24th Surah (An-Nur – "light"), which contains the words "Allah is the Light of the heavens and the earth". Many lamps of a similar type were made in Venice, on the island of Murano. Already during the Middle Ages, the island developed its own traditions of glass-making, producing objects exported by the Venetian republic not only to neighbouring European countries, but also to the entirety of Africa, Asia, and the Middle East. In the 17th century, when this lamp was made in Spain after a Murano specimen, the international fashion for Venetian glass was gradually coming to an end. It was replaced by a widespread fascination for the work of Bohemian craftsmen.

Lamp
North Africa, 18th century
FBQ. 8989 / Sheikh Faisal Bin Qassim Al Thani Museum

The Majlis: A Meeting Place   Exhibition

Ewer (Pitcher)
India, 18th century
FBQ. 7038 / Sheikh Faisal Bin Qassim Al Thani Museum

Jar
Kashan, Iran, 12th century
FBQ. 8985 / Sheikh Faisal Bin Qassim Al Thani Museum

Flask in polychrome ceramic with Saint George
Kütahya, Turkey, 18th century
Congregazione Armena Mechitarista, Monastero Armeno Mechitarista di San Lazzaro degli Armeni, Venezia

Drum (part of a theatre costume)
Syria, around 1894
Dutch National Museum of World Cultures

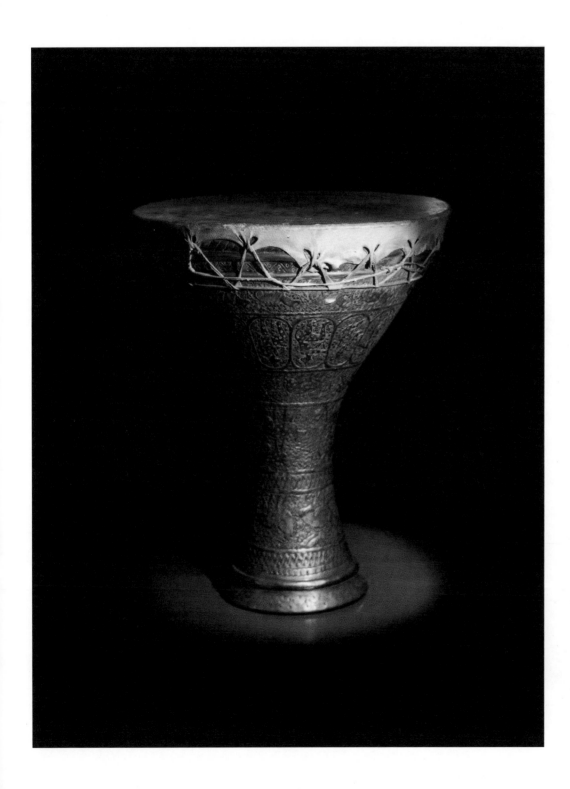

Ewer (Pitcher)
Uzbekistan, 17th century
FBQ. 6963 / Sheikh Faisal Bin Qassim Al Thani Museum

A Collection of Stories without Borders

Sheikh Faisal Bin Qassim Al Thani Museum (the FBQ Museum) is located in Al-Shahaniya municipality, Qatar, and hosts over 30,000 Islamic artefacts. The Museum has generously lent a great number of unique objects from its collection for the Majlis exhibition. Vera Trakhtenberg, a curator based in Moscow, travelled to Doha to speak with the staff of the museum about its collection and its cultural mission.

A Collection of Stories without Borders   57

VERA TRAKHTENBERG:

Claudio, tell us about the experience of working for the Sheikh Faisal Museum, which is new for you.

CLAUDIO CRAVERO,
Director of the Museum:

Being appointed director of the museum in December 2020 was a real challenge for me because I've always dealt with contemporary art, but at university I studied bioethics. The thought that every day I deal with incredible artefacts, as well as unique non-artistic materials, inspires me. When I see the beauty of these objects and learn their interesting histories, I ask myself how I should tell visitors about them the right way. After all, our exhibits come from different countries and eras, though their stories are still relevant today. Originally I saw photographs of the exhibition and thought that I needed to create some interactive displays in order to add some technology and modernity to the museum. But when I acquainted myself with the collection, in reality I was fascinated by how the narratives between objects are connected and how they all represent dots on a giant, single map. The museum founder's approach to the selection of exhibits reminds me of collections from the Renaissance era: collections of rarities and artefacts. This is the only optic we have for understanding how the FBQ Museum is organised. There's no need to introduce interactive technologies in order to improve some sections of the exhibition – it's better to make an interesting guide that allows

visitors to get a deeper understanding of the link between different exhibits. Our task is, first and foremost, to systematise the collection. In addition to this, we hold international exhibitions. Despite the pandemic, we have sent artefacts to different countries, gaining new international experience from exhibiting them.

VT: Jacob, how long have you been working at the museum? Tell us about the collection of Islamic art: what does it consist of, which items or artefacts have the most significant artistic and historical value, and how do they differ from other museums in the region?

JACOB VAN GULIK,
Assistant Curator of Islamic Art:

I've been working at the museum for more than three years. In fact, we're talking not about one, but about several Sheikh Faisal museums, since besides the building at the Al-Samriya farm in Al-Shahaniya, we also have a carpet museum on the sixth floor of the Marriott Marquis hotel in Doha's West Bay. On top of that, we're planning to open an automotive museum in the main building, which children will love for its interactive opportunities and which will tell the story of the development of transport, beginning with camels and ending with modern-day cars. The most important sections of the Sheikh Faisal collection are the swords and saddles, the artefacts made from wood, textiles, and jewellery, as well as a multitude of objects fashioned from mother-of-pearl and ivory. All these exhibits are found in the Islamic Art hall, from

Chess Box with Chess Pieces
Syria, 20th century
FBQ. 1081 and FBQ. 1081.1–2. / Sheikh Faisal Bin Qassim Al Thani Museum

where visitors then enter the Syrian House – a part of the museum that noticeably differs from the others. The special thing about this section of the exhibition is that, in 2014, the Syrian House was taken apart stone by stone in Damascus, shipped to Qatar, and then reassembled with the help of a carefully developed numeration system. What also amazes me in this part of the museum is that several decorative elements have more than a little in common with Egyptian architectural elements. Before entering the Syrian House, visitors are recommended to acquaint themselves with the collection of Morisco wheel-made ceramic plates and other types of artistically and calligraphically designed clayware. Within the collection of musical instruments, visitors can become familiar with the importance that is attached to culture, music, and other types of artistic expressions in Arabic culture. Right in front of the Syrian House is the Quran Room, or "House of the Quran", as it is literally named in Arabic. In this part of the museum, in itself a gem or highlight, is kept the world's smallest copy of the Quran and one of the biggest volumes of this sacred scripture. They both come from India, but the former was made in the nineteenth century and the latter a century earlier.

VT: Chady, how did your collaboration with the museum begin?

CHADY EL BAIK,
Carpet Museum Curator:

Twenty years ago, I came to Qatar and met His Excellency Sheikh Faisal for the first time. At that time, the museum was in a big Qatari fort and was just beginning its work. They asked me a very strange question: "What do I, as a representative of Arab culture, know about my history?" I realised that I didn't really know that much, and just several days later I became one of the happiest people in the world, since I got the opportunity to work personally with Sheikh Faisal and Professor Talib Al Baghdadi, who taught me everything that the museum embodies today. Each piece in our collection is a combination of art and craft. I enjoy discovering art objects in handicrafts and celebrating the skill of an artisan in works of art. I am looking for the beauty that is hidden in every object. I try to ensure that any artefact can "tell" its story to visitors. And, of course, I take good care of the exhibits, so that the next generation will have the chance to learn these stories.

VT: Waleed, you've been working at the museum for around nineteen years, and you've seen the formation of the collection, as well as its growth. Could you tell us about its past and near future?

WALEED AL DULAIMI,
Museum Curator:

From a closed private museum, we are moving towards becoming a museum of an international level, and preparing to welcome guests of the FIFA World Cup, which will take place in Qatar in 2022. We are constantly expanding the collection: it contains objects of different levels of complexity, representing different cultures. We also show parts of our collection in other countries. It is important that the collection of the

Sheikh Faisal Museum is constantly being added to. As of today, it numbers more than 30,000 items. The exhibits underline the importance of the cultural heritage not only of Qatar but of the entire Middle East region, as well as other parts of the world.

VT: I imagine that you've seen the changes that are taking place in Qatar as a result of the country's progressive development. Have attitudes towards traditions and heritage changed among the new generation?

WD: Qatar's leaders tell us that a museum is an institution for people of all ages, nationalities, and religions. At the same time, this museum was established in order to transport the past into the future, preserving the heritage and culture of our ancestors for our descendants.

VT: Jacob and Chady, which items from the Sheikh Faisal Museum collection do you consider the most interesting and important?

JG: The first thing that comes to mind is the copy of the key to the Kaaba in Mecca. The glass mosque lamps by Brocard and Chinese pottery intended for the Islamic market emphasise the range of our collection. The only really large object is a copy of the Aerospatiale Trinidad TB 20 Desert Princess aeroplane, which was personally flown by Sheikh Hamad bin Ali bin Jabor Al Thani. Seeing this object from certain angles and corners, and with the help of a little imagination, it is as if one pays a visit to an aviation museum in the Netherlands or a similar museum that I have seen myself in America some decades ago. Like the

National Museum of Qatar, we study the heritage of the country up until the "oil period" – the discovery of oil in Qatar in 1939 – but we are doing this in the context of Sheikh Faisal's personal collection. This feeling is strongest in the Rayyan room, which is devoted to hunting. Other parts of the exhibition include objects connected to falcon hunting, a section on dhow boats and pearl fishing, as well as a display devoted to camels. The last aspect connected with Qatari heritage that I would particularly like to highlight is the two Qatari houses inside the museum. In the small Qatari house you can find various kinds of cupboards and ceramics, and in the big one there are objects related to traditional Qatari ceremonies such as weddings, and the festival of Garangao, which is the night halfway through the Islamic fasting month of Ramadan, celebrated by children all over Qatar and other nations within the Gulf Region. During this celebration nuts and sweets are prepared, and the children's mothers stitch bags so that the children can collect the celebrational gifts they receive. Here, in the big Qatari house, you can also find items related to the time when Sheikh Faisal was still a child. In fact, there's absolutely no need to be an art connoisseur or an expert in order to love our museum, which has been built on a farm in Ash-Shahaniya, surrounded by numerous date palm plantations. When you are amid such natural, floral, and faunal diversity, you forget that you are in the centre of a country whose landscape is mainly desert.

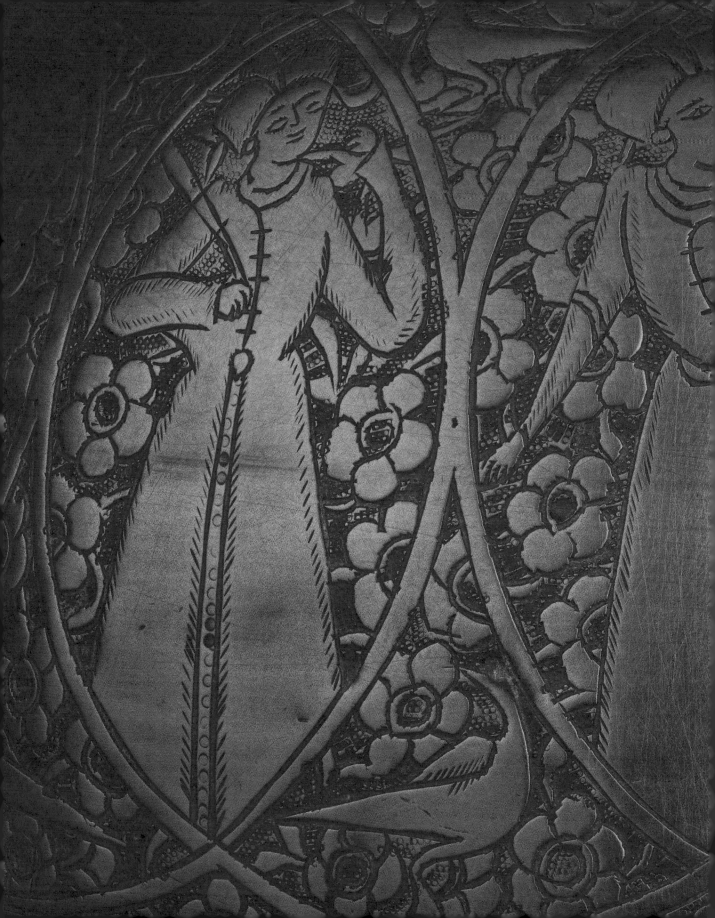

CB: A multitude of mysterious symbols, especially in tribal and religious contexts, can be found in our carpets and prayer rugs, which are on display in the West Bay branch of the museum. Exhibits like this don't have to be woven from silk or gold thread in order to have value. It could be a simple woollen carpet. However, it is unique and rare because, in the country where it was woven, carpets like that are no longer produced. In addition, any carpet could have been at an important meeting that changed the world, or where a peace agreement was signed. And this, undoubtedly, makes it valuable.

VT: Chady and Jacob, many cultures intersect in the Middle East, and sometimes come into conflict with each other, but contemporary Qatar is a place where different cultures and traditions exist in harmony. What does multiculturalism mean to you today, when the borders are closed, and we have limited freedom of movement?

CB: Qatar is flourishing in all spheres, primarily thanks to God and the wise government, led by His Highness Sheikh Tamim bin Hamad Al Thani, Amir of the State of Qatar. Our museum is a wonderful example of multiculturalism. We have representatives of more than fifteen nationalities working for us, and we all learn from each other. Despite the visible differences, you can find much in common between our cultures, which in the hard times that we are currently experiencing because of the pandemic helps us to overcome any difficulties together.

JG: I don't remember a large number of cultural clashes or conflicts. All similar phenomena in the Middle East come with emotions rooted in a certain life experience. It is impossible to gain a profound understanding of these processes by relying solely on books, articles, and encyclopaedias. Any museum provides visitors with direct contact with knowledge, and, in the end, this gives the opportunity to look with clearer eyes at what the media write about the intersection of cultures in the Middle East.

VT: One of the main difficulties for the artistic community in the Middle East concerns the use of narrative. Many practices, in which not only artists, curators, and writers, but also other creative people are engaged, are excluded from the global agenda but need to be visible. Claudio, in your opinion, what contribution could they make to the global art scene?

CC: Yes, this is a challenge that we need to talk about! The watershed was not the moment when oil was discovered, but when the events of September 11, 2001 spawned a wave of stereotypes about this region in the world's media. Similar over-simplified stereotypes existed already, but they were not as detrimental as in the period since 9/11. Around the same time, the Middle East gained access to the Internet, which gives access to a flux of information that had previously been inaccessible due to censorship. The most visited website across the Gulf region, for example, is YouTube because it represents a way of finding out what's going on abroad. As a result, creative people, like everyone else, are increasingly

Armour Shield
India, 18th century
FBQ. 1074 / Sheikh Faisal Bin Qassim Al Thani Museum

Palanquin (detail)
India, 19th century
FBQ. 523 / Sheikh Faisal Bin Qassim Al Thani Museum

exposed to the outside realm and more engaged with the international artistic context. This process has continued also thanks to Middle-East art fairs and the participation of artists in international biennials.

VT: It seems to me that one of the most important issues for artists in the region is their national identity. Recently they have gained the opportunity to study abroad, take part in international events or, at least, find out about the latest trends via the Internet. However, they don't imitate what they have seen, but invent their own artistic methods.

CC: Well, you've just formulated what I would call Middle Eastern identity. We have artists and curators who studied abroad, or have been able, in some sense, to culturally soak up international methodology. This new intelligentsia brought the lesson learnt abroad back to their own country by adapting foreign influences to the local context. And this brings us back to the question of what has to be done so that their voice can be heard in the world.

VT: Jacob, allow me to ask you a personal question: what is it like to be a European expat in modern-day Qatar?

JG: It's a very interesting experience, firstly from the point of view of moving around the city. I come from the Netherlands, a country that is famous for its pedestrian routes and bike lanes. Immediately after moving to Qatar, I thought about buying a bicycle, and I was advised by some of my neighbours to purchase one, but I then decided that it would be more convenient

to get around here on foot, like in my home country. Nonetheless, Doha does a lot for fans of cycling, and now they're building a big network of bike lanes here. In Amsterdam, it was habitual for me to go everywhere by bicycle, or I could always get on a train to get to any place in the country or within Europe, but in Qatar, everything's different. Here I feel that I'm dependent on public transport – but at the same time, I feel this gives me many opportunities to go around in Doha.

VT: Claudio, you began your career in Italy, where you studied the history of art and bioethics. Later, after working in Europe, you moved to the Gulf region. You worked as chief curator at the King Abdulaziz Centre for World Culture in Saudi Arabia and curator of fine arts at the Sheikh Abdullah Al-Salem Cultural Centre in Kuwait. What prompted you to move to this region?

CC: I was born in Italy, specialised in museum studies in France, and started working as a curator in Italy after training in New York. At some point, I felt I needed to explore something out of my comfort zone, and chances brought me to the Middle East in 2014. Back then, this region represented an uncharted territory I decided to embrace.

VT: Claudio and Jacob, what were your expectations before you left, and to what degree have they turned out to be justified after your move to the Middle East?

CC: Before I moved to the region, I barely knew where Saudi Arabia was, and I didn't have the slightest idea of what was in store for me in this part of the globe. After settling myself, I met many inspiring people who influenced my understanding of what is happening here, the historical context and today's ambitions. In French, the term for the Middle East is Moyen-Orient, which stands for "means". In French culture, the Middle East is a way (hence, a means) to reach the Far East. On the other hand, this region represents the centre that sits between East and West. And that's true! The Middle East is the centre of a broader region that sees the sun rising in China and set in the Maghreb, namely the West.

JG: One of the most unusual sensations in Qatar is that here you can be far away from nature and at the same time feel part of it. Another thing that initially surprised me, as a Dutchman, is the size of the cars. Later I understood that many native residents of the country need big vehicles like that for trips in the desert. On the whole, I adapted very well to the new living conditions, and I enjoy them.

VT: Claudio, one of the principles of your work is the decolonisation of the curatorial approach. How do you see decolonisation in the field of curation?

CC: In a certain sense, decolonising has become a trend, but, in essence, decolonisation is our only instrument for reinterpreting history. I can give an example: the branch of the Louvre in Abu Dhabi. How can we decolonise curation if the institution itself uses a colonial approach? However, we must give them their due, almost paving the

road with a set of guidelines for museums in the 21st century. The galleries at Louvre Abu Dhabi are not separated by geography but by chronological order. The works of art are juxtaposed, and, somehow, they overlap things that happened in several regions of the world at the same time, aiming at grabbing their specific zeitgeist. What stands out in this new presentation is that what was previously considered a specialised area of study, deemed as "marginal" or "ethnographic", is now investigated as a central narrative amongst the others. This approach expands on the assumed canons and allows us to avoid ghettoizing themes such as "black art", "queer art", "women's art", and so forth. I love decolonisation as the creation of a common context, in which the fixation on the local is less substantial than the vision of a general, international narrative in which everything is interconnected. The civic dimension in the role of today's curators plays a pivotal part in giving voice to unheard artists, as well as in questioning the functions that museums have to fulfil to close the gap between policy and practice in Western and non-Western art institutions.

Candle Holder
Egypt, 15th century
FBQ. 788. / Sheikh Faisal Bin Qassim Al Thani Museum

Craft Diplomacy: King Fuad's Khayamiya Textiles in a Dutch Museum

Dr Sarah Johnson, Middle East and North Africa Curator at the Dutch National Museum of World Cultures, describes the history of a particular set of textiles and points to the varying misunderstandings about their function and origins. She underlines the critical importance of the placement of these khayamiya in the Majlis exhibition, which are for the first time being displayed as an "architectural whole".

Craft Diplomacy

In September 1933, the Egyptian King Fuad I (1868–1936) sent a set of 13 textiles as a diplomatic gift to the Oosters Institute in the Netherlands. These 2.4-metre-tall textiles were a form of cotton appliqué called khayamiya in Arabic (page 73). Members of the Oosters Instituut hung a few of these textiles on the walls of their headquarters as part of a small museum display, with various other gifts and objects collected by the institute. When the institute loaned the gifts indefinitely to the Museum Volkenkunde in Leiden in 1958, the textiles were mistakenly labelled as "Arabian", and they disappeared into storage until a curator noticed them again in 2016. Why was this gift of important textiles forgotten?

A photograph of this diplomatic exchange provides a clue. A board member of the Oosters Instituut stands on one of the textiles, which is sprawled on the floor like a carpet, between two wooden Quran stands (page 74). Behind him, another textile is draped over a table, like a table cloth, with metal bowls and plates piled on top. Next to the table, the Egyptian ambassador, Murad Kamil Bey, and another board member of the Institute, Christiaan Snouck Hurgronje (1857–1936), look on. The focus is on the political actors, rather than on the textiles themselves.

Egypt became independent in 1922 and its leaders were looking for identity markers for the new nation. Khayamiya was an obvious choice for one of the new nation's symbols. The textiles were a legacy from Ottoman tentmaking, but the appliqué work and patterns were unique to the Egyptian context. In a photograph from 1927, King Fuad sits in front of his cere-

monial khayamiya tent during the opening of the Egyptian Spinning and Weaving Company (page 77). By the late nineteenth century, khayamiya textiles were also widely collected and displayed by Europeans and Americans. The tentmakers who produced the textiles in Cairo started shifting their production to accommodate this new market. They made smaller khayamiya with scenes from ancient Egypt, or even from tourist photography, to tailor to European and American tastes. These textiles were often used as backdrops at the Egyptian area of world exhibitions in Europe.

Some wealthier collectors purchased larger panels or whole tents. These were sometimes displayed as wall hangings, closer to their original Egyptian context. Henri Matisse, for example, was photographed by Henri Cartier-Bresson in front of his khayamiya panel. But for most Europeans and Americans at the time, the fascination with these textiles was more in the craftsmanship of the appliqué textile work than in their vernacular architecture function within Egyptian society. This was partly due to the interest of many Euro-American institutions at the time in the Orientalist idea of finding handmade crafts outside of Europe and America, which could be used to mark the contrast between the "industrialised world" and the less modern "other". For example, Captain T.C. Speedy collected a khayamiya panel during the British campaign in Abyssinia in 1867–68, which was installed horizontally rather than vertically in the British Museum, making the Arabic calligraphy impossible to read.

The khayamiya textiles Fuad gave to the Oosters Instituut were never used in

Egypt but made specifically for this diplomatic exchange. The calligraphy and design appealed to the taste of a group of highly-educated Dutch men who studied the Arabic language and Islam as their profession. The textiles have Quranic inscriptions, which were rare in Egypt by the 1930s. The colour scheme of blues, reds, and yellows, as well as the elaborate floral patterns, hark back to an earlier period of design in the late nineteenth and early twentieth century. In this period, these patterns, drawn from medieval forms of the Mamluk Empire, were popular both among tourists and Egyptians.

As "imitations", can these textiles still provide the contemporary viewer with an understanding of the vernacular context in which khayamiya are used? Or should they provide an architectural context at all? These textiles continue to be a ubiquitous form of vernacular architecture in Egypt today. They are used across all levels of society as tents to celebrate important events, such as weddings and funerals. But they are seen mainly as architecture, not as craft, and are rarely displayed in museums in Egypt.

The Majlis exhibition presents one possibility for restoring the architectural element to these textiles. For the first time in their history, these khayamiya are displayed as an architectural whole, creating an enclosed room or tent in the exhibition. Also, the main feature of the exhibition, a contemporary tent, is used as an active gathering space rather than a roped-off museum display, reminding the visitor of the social function of such textiles. These two tents build on one another: the khayamiya,

overtly political, reminding us of the diplomatic negotiations of all such global cultural endeavours, and the contemporary tent forefronting the makers over the political actors. The focus in Majlis on the Moroccan weavers who produced the wool textiles for the contemporary tent reminds us of the anonymity of the tentmakers who made the 1933 khayamiya. Hopefully, this display of khayamiya in the Majlis exhibition can also shift the focus from the king to the tentmaker in the story of khayamiya.

King Fuad I of Egypt sitting inside a ceremonial tent set up in the
Cotton Spinning and Weaving Company at El-Mahalla El-Kubra, 1927.
Photograph by Riad Shehata

Protecting Power of the Written Word

Athens-born artist Irini Gonou creates works that heal and protect. Her pieces that employ ancient Arabic calligraphy have been shown in Greece, Cyprus, France, Germany, UK, Belgium, USA, Norway, and Egypt. Here, she speaks about the symbolism and meaning of her work for the Majlis and the value of tradition.

LESIA PROKOPENKO:

Could you briefly describe the idea behind your work and what you personally wanted to achieve with it?

IRINI GONOU:

My work is called the Majlis Banner. It's a work to honour the desert. The word "Majlis" on the front of the piece is written in square Kufic script. In Arabic, Majlis stands for a meeting place where people get together. Square Kufic calligraphy is a particular style of script from the 8th century BCE, widely used in architecture. Because it's an architectural Biennale – and the Majlis is a piece of architecture – the materials I used are bamboo and textile, the same materials the Majlis was constructed with. So I tried to stay in the same mood.

I used cotton fabric with all-natural dyes: I tried to find the colour of the desert for the background. As a natural element, the desert inspires us with its simplicity, purity, and austerity. The red-coloured word "Majlis" in the middle of the artwork is a kind of patchwork made of ancient silk fabrics, reminiscent of the traditional use of tiles for Kufic script. On the rear side of the piece, we can find twelve hidden amulets – amuletic words written in square Kufic calligraphy and hand-printed in the linocut technique; they provide the Majlis Banner with the properties of a large amulet. These words are some of the names of Allah, but also the highest qualities in the human world: the Eternal, the Beautiful, the Light, the Generous, the All-Subtle, the Beloved, the Giver of All, the Patient, the All-Wise, Love, Health, and Peace.

L: Your works are mainly aimed at healing and protection. How does this work?

I: It comes from an ancient Mediterranean belief that script had healing and protecting powers. In the Arabic world this could be texts from the Quran, the words of God. A lot of Islamic art pieces are based on that concept. So I used the names of God, but also the names of love because in the Arabic culture there are fifty names for love. And I feel that writing the names of love is universal – it's something we all need, something our society needs to work on. I write these words on reeds: in the Arabic world, reed has always been the traditional implement for writing – the Qalam. I attach the reeds I write on to the fabric or other material and it becomes a protective or a healing object. I use the Kufic script because for me it links the past with the present. It is in fact an ancient script but visually it has a very contemporary form.

L: And what is important for you as an artist at the moment? What are you working on?

I: It is very important for me to preserve the tradition: not just keeping it in a museum, but using it, reusing it, making it active, and keeping it alive. To give it a new life today. In my concept of using the script as a protective element, that means reactivating a very old cultural belief. I also like to promote natural materials because I believe that nature heals. The plants I use to make the dyes are also medicinal, they offer us numerous benefits. So, we have all this good energy around us, coming from

nature – and this is something we have to keep thinking about, making it active and vibrant. This is my method.

L: And how did you arrive at it? How did you begin doing this kind of work?

I: I've been making art since 1974. I attended the École nationale supérieure des Beaux-Arts and the École nationale supérieure des arts décoratifs in Paris, and have been working as an artist ever since. I passed through different paths before arriving at what I'm doing now, but I've always been attracted to nature and natural materials. At some point I realised that Western civilisation was missing the elements that I later found in other cultures, particularly North African and Middle Eastern, as well as in Persian, Indian, and Chinese cultures. This study and creative process has been enriching, leading me towards new collaborations and artistic journeys.

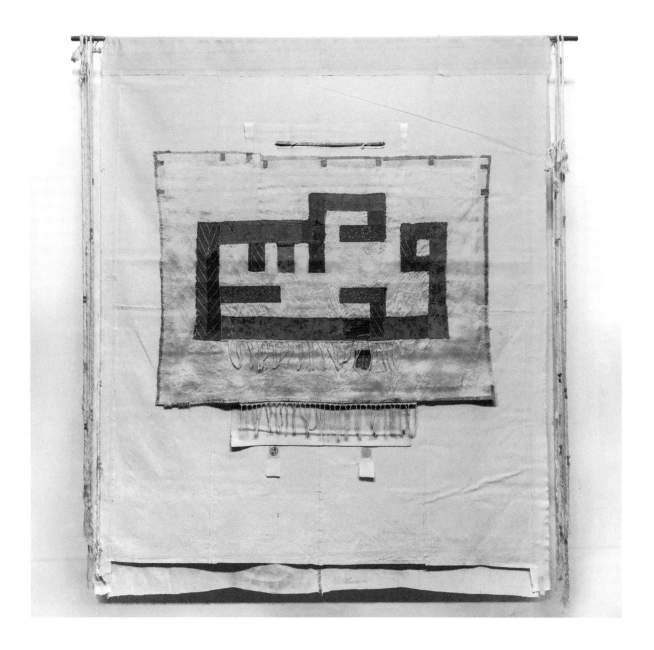

Jörg Gruber on Documenting Craft

Jörg Gruber is an acclaimed photographer and cinematographer who has been documenting the working process of craftspeople connected to Caravane Earth's initiatives, in particular, those responsible for the construction of the Majlis. He speaks about his working process, impressions from the field, and the intersection of craft and creativity.

BEN WHEELER:

What are some of the challenges for you as a photographer trying to capture the process of labour and craft?

JÖRG GRUBER:

I think the major point is always the time – how much time you spend with people. When you are photographing and documenting work, you must do so in a way that makes it clear to the viewer how the process works, and this needs time. So it makes no sense, in my opinion, to go to a weaver and just to film them for five minutes. All the people we visited with Caravane – workers, artists, and artisans – they were all very interesting and very regular, welcoming people. It was easy to photograph them as they were very open. But I think the biggest mistake you can make is to focus on these meetings and then you have no time to film the actual process.

B: What surprised you about your experiences in these different communities?

J: I was most surprised by the sheer amount of patience that people have. We went, for example, to India to visit silk weavers. It's unbelievable. The material is so thin and delicate and the process takes a long time. These people have incredible patience with the process. That's one aspect that impressed me. Another was something I experienced photographing carpet makers in Morocco. These women, they are sitting day after day, paying such close attention to these details – and they love their work! In

some areas they were sitting in places with no heating systems, working with bad light, and they're actually happy. The women in Morocco, and especially the cooperative we spent time in, from them I got the impression that this was one of the best times of their lives. Now they have built this cooperative and they can, for example, pay their own bills. They have bank accounts and cards – it seems they are quite happy to take an active role in improving their own lives. It's also very communal – they are sitting together in a room and chatting all day. They eat together, they have tea together. It's a community.

B: As a photographer, do you consider what you do "craft"? And if so, did you feel a particular affinity for these craftspeople, and did they feel something similar towards you?

J: Craft is part of it, there's a creation moment. The same with cinematography – when you are filming, you first have to know your craft and then you can start to be free and be creative. And I do think there was a kind of recognition from my side and the side of the craftspeople about the work we were both doing. When we're doing this documentary shooting there's a lot to do, it's really hard labour. You're running around, carrying stuff, sweating – in different climates and different countries. You have to work, work, work, and the craftspeople do see it and I think respect it.

Worker on the Bamboo plantation El Quindío
Colombia, 2019

The Majlis: A Meeting Place Exhibition

Fatima Chimiti, Weaver
Boujad, Morocco, 2019

The Majlis: A Meeting Place   Exhibition

Ahmed Chmiti, Master Tent Maker and Weaver of the Majlis
Boujad, Morocco, 2019

Aisha Fadili, Weaver
Boujad, Morocco, 2019

The Majlis: A Meeting Place   Exhibition

Architecture

The structure of the Majlis illustrates a multi-layered heritage. It is a critical example of an approach to architecture that is practised with an open mind and mutual respect towards the past and future. So often, the inherent potential of an inclusive, forward-looking architecture is often overshadowed by the ever-growing construction of utilitarian structures that reject what has come before. Architecture is among the most tangible expressions of Western design dominance, as concrete, glass, and steel have replaced textile, wood, and earth at a societal and environmental cost that is difficult to measure. It is also a palpable sign of indigenous cultures disappearing; cultures whose identity relies on co-existence with nature. Urban development tactics of today risk alienating individuals from culture and nature, ultimately undermining solidarity among peoples.

To counter these disturbing trends, multiple initiatives of Caravane Earth work to bring the practice of architecture closer to the realm of communal and cross-cultural engagement. Whether it is through the foundation of an essential archive of architectural materials, the planning and drafting of completely new forms of habitation, or the research of indigenous materials and practices, Caravane Earth is elevating and supporting changes to architectural approaches without stripping them of their essential humanity. With the Majlis, we are paying homage to tradition, to localities, to innovation, to collaboration, and to individual visions.

Caravane Earth's Art Village

Many of the original ideas and inspirations for the activities of Caravane Earth can be drawn back to the Art Village: the foundation's flagship concept. Designed for arid and semi-arid environments, this research included a framework for a type of village that would be assembled annually and in a variety of potential locations – a place for human beings to gather, exchange knowledge, and develop skills for living on Earth. It was meant as a place to cultivate interconnectivity between the thoughts, words, and actions we need to live with ourselves, each other, and nature.

Critical work for the village included a workshop series led by Natalya Orekhova and Andrey Sviridov of the organisation CXEMA, which was delivered in July 2019 in Moscow to a group of architecture students from the Design and Architecture Academies of Moscow. The aim was to encourage students to think differently about architecture and the concept of "home" and to reflect on the sacred interconnectivity between Humans, Culture, and Nature. Students were asked to design homes that worked in harmony with a desert environment, taking a holistic approach, using sustainable materials and techniques. They were asked to research and then design a solution for the desert and then to prototype some of the ideas.

The Majlis itself stems from these instances of initial research. The Art Village was the first point of connection between Caravane Earth and the team of Colombian architects Simón Vélez and Stefana Simic. Their organisation in Bogota, Gigagrass, was involved in the initial development of the plans for the village. The experiments and trials with the villages' structures also paved the way for what would later become the material for the Majlis. Textiles originating in the Bedouin tradition of folding buildings for transport were incorporated after bamboo decoration was found to be too heavy.

Thus the connection between Colombian bamboo and Moroccan textiles was formed. The concept did indeed cultivate interconnectivity as originally intended, the results of which can be witnessed today in the form of the Majlis at the 2021 Venice Biennale.

CARAVANE

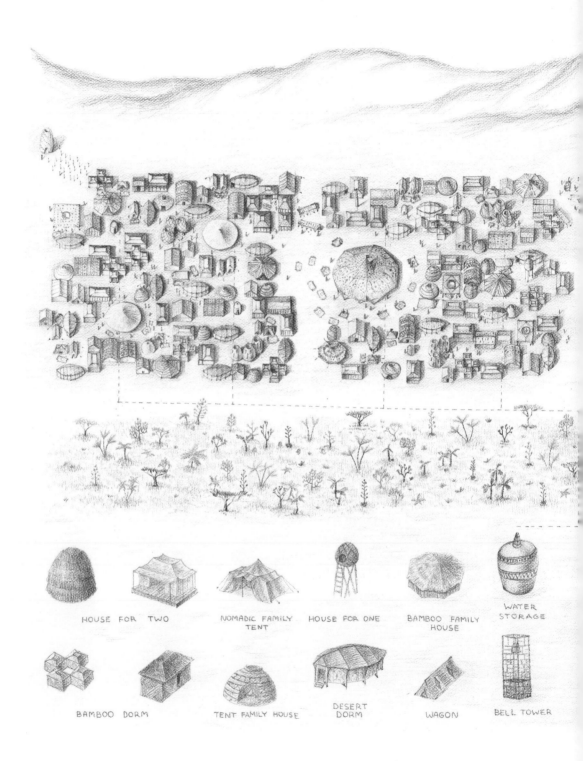

HOUSE FOR TWO

NOMADIC FAMILY TENT

HOUSE FOR ONE

BAMBOO FAMILY HOUSE

WATER STORAGE

BAMBOO DORM

TENT FAMILY HOUSE

DESERT DORM

WAGON

BELL TOWER

MASTERPLAN

N

KITCHEN

WORKSHOP

THEATRE

MUSIC
SEMINARY

MAJILIS

SILENT ROOM

WC

CAMEL SHADE

STORAGE

ADMINISTRATION
REMOTE

WI-FI HUB

Caravane Earth Art Village

The Majlis: A Meeting Place   Architecture

The Path of Bamboo with Simón Vélez and Stefana Simic

Colombian architect Simón Vélez is the world's foremost innovator working with bamboo, the most sustainable of natural building materials. Together with Stefana Simic, a project architect from New York, they run the Bogota-based international design atelier GIGAGRASS. Researcher Alexander Ostrogorsky explores the present-day relevance of bamboo architecture and tells the story of Simón and Stefana's committed contribution to its development.

Manizales, Colombia. Place.
Panamericana Highway

If you drink coffee, there is a one in ten chance that it is made from beans grown in Colombia. If your coffee is indeed from Colombia, then it is almost certainly produced in the Coffee Triangle – a group of areas in the western part of the country in the foothills of the Andes, designated by UNESCO as a World Heritage region due to the uniqueness of its natural, cultural, and agricultural features.

Manizales is one of the major cities in the Triangle, located on a hillside at 2,000 metres above sea level. Narrow streets run up or down the hill at sharp angles. Only a few quarters have houses more than three or four storeys high, although the city is not that small – it is home to half a million inhabitants. In addition to being one of the centres of coffee production, the city is also known as an educational centre, housing several universities. Every tenth Manizalean you meet on the streets is a student or a university teacher. If neither coffee nor education appeal to you, you might still be interested in the local theatre or jazz festivals – the first to be held in the country and some of the largest in the region – or in the January fair with its bullfighting, horse races, and parades.

If you take the Panamericana highway from Bogota, and are a few kilometres away from the city, then, passing by gas stations, warehouses, and rest stops for long-haul truck drivers, you ought not to miss a right turn, leading to the Recinto del Pensamiento park. In the "Garden of Contemplations" – a possible translation of this name into English – you will find a greenhouse with orchids and a pavilion with butterflies, but also a hotel, and some good coffee – which is unsurprising, not only because the park is located in a coffee-producing region, but also because the park is owned by the local association of coffee producers. The taste could disappoint though: the best beans are exported, and the coffee you drink at home might not be available in its homeland. But we are interested in something else anyway.

The park appeared in the 1930s, when Manizales was a very small town, and a very young one – several large fires that occurred within an interval of a couple of years left only a few 19th-century buildings and landmarks standing in their wake. Where the park now stands, there was a school built for local orphaned children. The school's programme could be called progressive – for those times and in this region, teaching and feeding children was a certain way to get relatively high results. Now only the name of the park reminds us of this past. And there is one more thing here – a circular bamboo pavilion in the furthest corner of the territory, on the fringe of a forest, an exercise in progressive construction technology. The circular building looks like an overturned woven fruit basket or a funny hat. And yet, the supports, placed at a slight angle, and a very prominent portico give it a clear, dynamic silhouette. Although bamboo is one of the oldest construction materials, the pavilion looks neither archaic, nor simple. Indeed, the technology used in its construction is itself not quite simple at all.

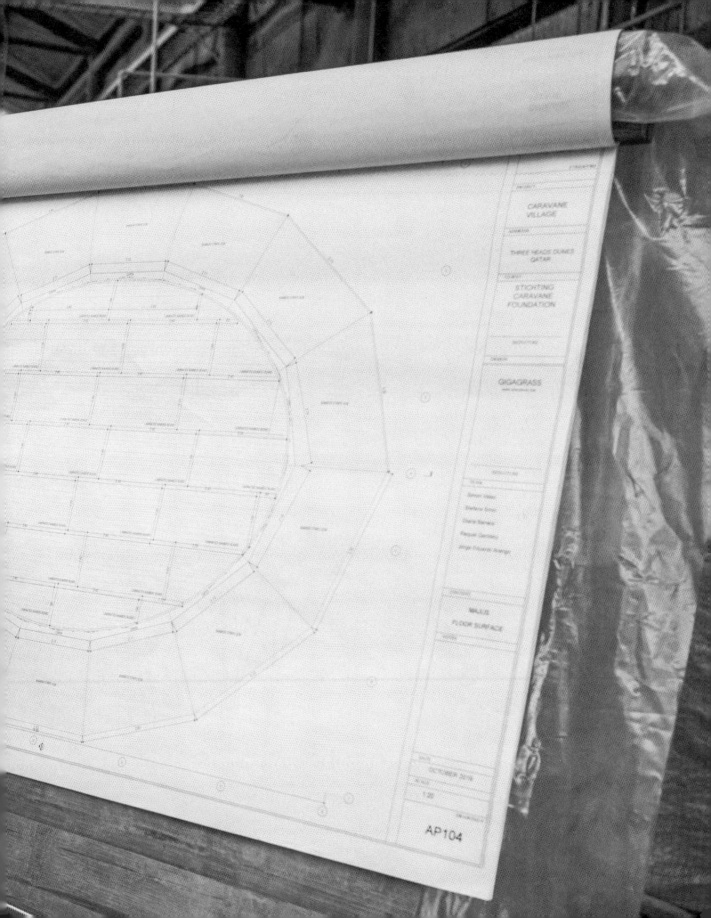

Hannover, Germany.
Construction. The Rights of Grass

The pavilion was designed by the architect Simón Vélez, a native of Manizales, now however living predominantly in the capital along with his wife and Gigagrass design atelier partner Stefana Simic. The pavilion was built in 1999 on the initiative of the ZERI (Zero Emissions Research and Initiatives) international network of ecological projects. At the Expo 2000 in Hannover, dedicated to green technologies, Vélez and his ZERI colleagues were to demonstrate the potential of bamboo as an ecological construction material, easily accessible for millions of people living in poverty-stricken regions of the planet.

The pavilion at the "Garden of Contemplations" was built by Simón Vélez a little earlier; German authorities were not ready to give their permission for building an innovative construction of that size, and some proof – we could call it a full-scale model – was needed. The pavilion was part of a story told about an exemplary farming enterprise developed by ZERI – a farm which uses natural resources effectively and depends not only on coffee production, as coffee is a very delicate product, with unfortunate weather circumstances or global market fluctuations often leading farmers to the brink of bankruptcy.

Of course, Vélez was invited not because he is a native of Manizales. His father and grandfather worked with wood, and Símon even now collaborates with artisans whose ancestors worked with his own. But he moved away from wood and towards bamboo, perfecting the technology of working with it, making the already firm material even harder. The pavilion in Hannover and its clone in Manizales made his approach known to the whole world, but they are far from the only experiments. Vélez has built churches in Pereira and Cartagena in Colombia, a museum in Mexico City, a spa hotel in China, and tens of other buildings from bamboo, large and small.

He could have built even more, and what stops him is not so much the interest of customers or the capacities of the material, but the legal restrictions enforced on architects and builders. Vélez calls it "botanical colonialism" – a set hierarchy for materials and technologies, built upon the notions of the European man concerning what is sturdy and acceptable for construction, and what is not and has merit only for temporary constructions or decoration. And yet, almost all publications discussing bamboo as a construction material mention Vélez and his experiments. In 2016, when the Architecture Biennale was curated by the Chilean architect Alejandro Aravena, who chose for it the theme of "Reporting from the Front", he allotted one of the curatorial exhibition rooms especially for Vélez, along with the Russian Alexander Brodsky, the Swiss Peter Zumtor, the Japanese Kengo Kuma and many other architects, some famous and some relatively new in the public eye. Five years later, Vélez returned to Venice with a pavilion for the Majlis project, piercing through the very essence of contradictions between modern and traditional, professional and vernacular, industrial and artisanal.

Venice, Italy.
Technology. Unfreemasons

The Venice Architecture Biennale is the main event of the architecture establishment, its poster child and a manifestation of the architectural profession's immersion into itself. Every two years a curator chooses a topic and organises an exhibition at the Arsenale. Exhibitions interpreting the topic in their own way also spring up at the national pavilions and the Giardini gardens. A certain unclear rhythm can be glimpsed in the succession of agendas. Topics, aimed at the community and the discipline, such as David Chipperfield's "Common Ground" in 2012 and Rem Koolhaas' "Fundamentals" in 2014, are followed by manifests which propose to break out of the constraints of the strictly professional and towards the problems of the real world. Such was Alejandro Aravena's "Reporting from the Front" at the 2016 Biennale, which Simon Vélez also took part in.

The 17th Biennale was also meant to be like that, with its topic "How will we live together?", posed by the curator Hashim Sarkis – a native of Lebanon who moved to the West rather early in his life, beginning his architectural practice in the USA and now heading the MIT School of Architecture – sounding like both a very timely and modern and a perennial question. What is a house and a city, if not a means of living together? And is it not now that we most doubt humanity's capacity for cooperation?

The topic was meant to start a conversation between professionals about the problems civilisation is facing. But first, an eruption of reality into the cosy intellectual and artistic universe of the Biennale happened: the pandemic made the concerns raised by the topic a lot more acute. It turned out that the progress to peaceful and flourishing coexistence is hindered not only by political conflict, but also, it seems, by the powers of nature, although also translated into human demands and medical-policing norms.

The exhibition was postponed by a year, breaking the rhythm which had remained unbroken for three centuries. When the Biennale finally opened, it turned out to be a lot less crowded and rich than before, but a lot more present in the virtual world. The curatorial teams themselves, obliged to attend, were the main audience of the exhibitions – a mockery of the closed-off cliquishness typical of the event, criticised more and more frequently.

The Majlis project, initiated by Caravane Earth, fits the theme of the Biennale rather well, giving it some definition. The indifferent "together" which is supposed to inform our ability to "live" in the curatorial question are here replaced by more concrete roles: those of a host and a guest. In the context of the Biennale, this metaphor remains open to interpretation (but still not as open as the general formulation of the topic). Maybe the architect is the owner of the pavilion, while all the others are guests? Or maybe it is the other way around, and the architect is a guest to those, for whom he or she designs? Or maybe we are all guests and hosts for each other when we make contact with cultures new to us? But the list of the project's participants points to yet another reading: tradition, locality, handicraft and modernity, globalisation, production – some of those are guests, while the others are hosts.

The relationship of host and guest is individualised in principle, slowed by the compliance with rules and rituals. This distinguishes them from food and drink establishments or hotels, where, it may seem, something akin to hospitality unfolds (the sector is even called that). This is reminiscent of the distinction between handicraft and technology. The series of actions, leading to a certain object appearing in the hands of a craftsman, can be, at first glance, identical to that which leads to the object being made in a factory. But in the workshop many things can influence the outcome, making one object different from another, while in the factory, everything is thought through to make the objects identical.

Handicraft, however, is not merely arbitrary, an artistic practice in the romantic sense – after all, it bears within itself the energy and framework of tradition. And, unlike in technology, in tradition the fundamentals of culture and value are always present more manifestly, and it is impossible to avoid holding a constant dialogue within these fundamentals. The process of manufacturing a thing becomes the space for this dialogue, encompassing that which the craftsman learns, the knots and decisions suggested to him by tradition, as well as what remains open to interpretation in response to the demands of the circumstances or as a manifestation of individual taste. All of this can be read as a tale about the past and the present – all the more when there is a community, so that not only the system of material decisions is preassigned, but a choreography of interaction, filled with its own dramatic composition.

Colombia, Again. Faveoli. Factors of Progress

Amos Rapoport, a scholar of vernacular architecture, remarks in his 1969 book House Form and Culture that material, construction, and technology are all "modifying" factors. Unlike culture and climate, they do not determine the shape of a house, but only point to the boundaries of the possible in the actualisation of that archetype, which was formed in response to the demand of natural conditions and the social environment. Builders rooted in tradition were confronted with the accessibility of a certain material that needed to be handled in a certain way. They had to find responses to certain situations, but always strove to achieve the results they were after, namely: a building shape and layout corresponding to the climate conditions and the way of life in the family and the community. That said, the conventional solutions tended to migrate past these cultural boundaries. Moves resembling the traditional were used in "high art" and, conversely, technologies and elements from the professional arsenal found their way into "architecture without architects" (a term proposed around Rapoport's time by the scholar Bernard Rudofsky).

And yet it is difficult to imagine the process by which technologies of collective construction migrate. In this construction, the community is organised to produce material, assemble the construction, build the walls and lay down floors and ceilings –

a tradition one can encounter in all parts of the world. Rapoport remarks that this kind of interaction presupposes a certain connection between social organisation (who participates, how the roles are distributed, who leads) and the technological process (for example, whether the construction happens on site or whether the fragments of the house are assembled in advance and then installed on the construction plot). In any case, the meaning of this connection lies in the distribution of resources and responsibility. Neither fame, nor reward for work, nor especially expensive material and complex technologies are concentrated in the hands of the customer, builders, or the author of the project.

Here Rapoport finds unexpected common ground with Gottfried Semper, a mid-nineteenth century theoretician of architecture and design. Reflecting on the massive speed of progress, he proposed a rather original theory of the relation between architecture and technology, in which the latter plays a determining role. Methods used in stoneworking, woodworking, pottery and tailoring seemed to him to form the basis of constructive and aesthetic decisions, characteristic for corresponding epochs and regions. Now, after several sharp turns taken by architecture in its development, the measure of simplicity, characteristic for this theory, no longer looks as naive.

Unlike Rapoport, Semper was less interested in those forms of social organisation which could influence the forms of architecture – or rather, he thought of them in a somewhat mythological key. And yet the sense of community entered his theory in a completely unexpected context   in his reflections on the task which could be resolved only through the common effort of craftsmen, artists, architects, industrialists: the task of reconceptualising the relations between art and mass production.

At the end of the day, Semper immersed himself into craft in order to justify the persuasiveness and vitality of the architecture of our forebears. In our time, this looks like an interesting commentary to the desensibilisation effect which technology exerts on architecture.

We cannot speak of locality now: the methods of construction in general belong to the West, while materials are largely produced in developing countries. The same thing can be said about the ratio of architectural management and labour power. But in the process of globalisation, they are mixed. The peculiarities of climate and culture, the habits and tastes of craftsmen do not play a decisive role. Technology becomes definitive, offering a unified form to every context, and not only when it comes to large buildings built by famous architects.

Colombia is facing a housing crisis. After many years of civil war and an equally violent war against drug cartels, around a third of its population live in slums. In the architectural sense, a slum is an organism that grows and transforms itself in response to the growing number of inhabitants and a change in their needs.

The birth of a child, a wedding, the start of a new business or the closure of a bankrupt one, death, divorce – the material structure can react quickly and flexibly to all changes in civil and economic state.

The most prevalent construction materials in the favelas, as in most informal settlements in the world, inhabited by almost a seventh of the world population, are not of natural origin. They rather belong to second nature, whose offerings flood the building material markets with profusion – brick, tile, plaster. Those materials imply the formation of favose and fractionary structures: here's a room, another one is tacked next to it, a third room on top, and so on. There is no place for complicated calculation and constructions uniting several spaces with a single system of wall or ceiling here. There is no need for cooperation: laying brick is an exercise one person could get through, with the appearance of a second speeding up the process without substantially changing it. The discreteness of the material space is mirrored by the torn-ness of the social, i.e. the senses of closedness, isolation, hostility, characteristic for such a way of life. Within the favose structure, various alliances, unions and groups emerge, radio stations and cultural centres operate, but the inhabitants of two neighbouring faveoli could very well not know and fear each other. Technology becomes a metaphor and a reflection of the social, just like Rapoport wrote. It determines the aesthetics and pragmatics – as Semper pointed out – and enshrines one of the most widespread means of living together today.

Venice, Again.
Knots. Garden Pavilion

The pavilion in the park in Manizales is built from guadua bamboo. It is one of the almost 150 varieties of the plant which grow in tropical and subtropical regions of Asia, Oceania, and South America – in all parts of the world except Europe. Varieties of bamboo differ in thickness, speed of growth, and flexibility. It grows to be up to 30 metres in height and the diameter of the stems can reach 20 centimetres. After three or four years of growth, bamboo stalks become as hard as wood, and then it is time to use them in construction.

Constructions made from bamboo can compare to those of steel when it comes to sturdiness. But they are significantly lighter, which lets people raise rather impressively-sized buildings without using any technology. Long stalks play the role of load-bearing constructions – thrusts and trusses. Shorter and more flexible ones can be used to weave walls and roofs. Bamboo can be used to make regular flat planks or plywood. Bamboo is the material of choice in seismically hazardous zones also because of its elasticity, which absorbs the impact of tremors.

The material has its own shortcomings – it needs to be protected from mould, insects, and, obviously, fire with the help of special treatments. The alternative is to constantly replace damaged fragments and reconstruct buildings, which does not vex anyone in traditional cultures, not concerned with problems of authenticity and authorship. As a result, in rural areas of many countries, bamboo is used in half of all the constructions or even more; it is no coincidence that it is called "the poor man's wood".

Simón Vélez, architect, son, and grandson of architects, discovered the capacities of bamboo already as a young man. Later, he was joined by Stefana Simic, educated at the University of Columbia in the USA. As partners and spouses, they started the Gigagrass design atelier – a name which speaks to their main interest, the gigantic grass, which can be more sturdy than wood, lighter than steel and harder than concrete.

Researchers know of thousands of different traditional means of construction with bamboo, as well as many modifications, achieved with the use of modern materials. In the Hannover pavilion project, Simón Vélez and German engineers used the technique of filling bamboo pipes with cement, which made them extra sturdy.

But the material was not the only thing they borrowed from traditional architecture. First, the effective use of bamboo almost always means coordinated work by several people. Elasticity, one of the most useful features of this grass, manifests itself especially well in constructions which are under tension. Their building requires interaction, just like when setting up a large tent. Construction material turns out to be the foundation of a community.

Second, in their buildings you can often see a reference to traditional archetypes of space. At the core of many of them, there is the idea of a gathering which requires a spacious hall. A large roof is not only a defence against the burning sun and heavy rain, characteristic of the tropics, but a means to make a fragment of the earth stand out, pointing to its significance. Therein lies the monumental character of vernacular architecture, to which marble and sophisticated decorations are inaccessible: its ability to unite a large group of people, to serve not one family, but an entire village.

This is also true of the building constructed for the Majlis project: a round pavilion with a concourse and a cupola, a bamboo frame sheathed in Moroccan hand-woven textile, produced by a co-operative of women-weavers. It stands in the courtyard of a Benedictine monastery, in the middle of a garden designed by the landscape architect Todd Longstaffe-Gowan.

The pavilion houses an exhibition answering the Biennale's main question, "How will we live together?", prepared with objects from the Dutch National Museum of World Cultures and the Sheikh Faisal Bin Qassim Al Thani Museum in Qatar.

Documenting Architectural Tradition

Abdel-Wahed El-Wakil is a renowned Islamic architect. Caravane Earth is proud to be incubating a special educational programme that will focus on preserving the archive, legacy, and knowledge of the life and work of this master architect. Here, we are publishing archival materials that will be featured in an upcoming documentary on his life and work that was filmed and produced by Caravane Earth.

1	Entrance portico	16 Lobby
2	Doorman	17 Family room
3	Majlis	18 Master bedroom
4	Kitchen	19 Atrium
5	Bedroom	20 Bath
6	Entry	21 Dressing
7	Living room	22 Pergola
8	Main entrance	23 Bedroom
9	Library	24 Bridge/gallery
10	Gallery	25 Swimming pool
11	Q'aa	26 Kitchen
12	Roshan	27 Pergola
13	Salamlik	28 Servants' quarters
14	Dining room	
15	Pantry	

Ground Floor Plan

Corniche Mosque, 1986
Jeddah, Saudi Arabia

Documenting Architectural Tradition

Halawa House, 1975
Agamy, Egypt

Miqat Mosque Complex, 1987
Abyar 'Ali (Medina), Saudi Arabia

Documenting Architectural Tradition

Island Mosque, 1986
Jeddah, Saudi Arabia

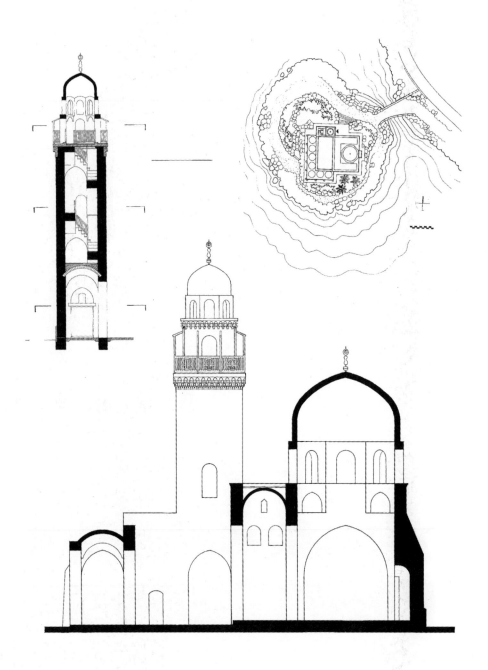

The Majlis: A Meeting Place   Architecture

A Network For Preserving Tradition

The International Network for Traditional Building, Architecture & Urbanism (INTBAU) is a global network that promotes traditional building, architecture, and urbanism. They will take part in a Caravane Earth event in Venice during which they will give an introduction to their community of researchers. Harriet Wennberg, Executive Director at INTBAU, discusses three of their projects that clearly illustrate what was good yesterday definitely should not be forgotten today.

FURQAT PALVAN-ZADE:

In your text "Urban Fusion" in which you describe INTBAU's approach, you talk about the false dichotomy of modern and traditional. Could you expand on this contradiction and share your thoughts on how our cities and societies could preserve cultural traditions while constantly moving forward?

HARRIET WENNBERG:

In this piece I am criticising the distinction that's often drawn between the modern and the traditional – when something "traditional" is described as necessarily related to the past or to something preserved in aspic. And that's not what tradition as a concept has ever intended or evolved to be. Gustav Mahler once defined tradition as keeping the flame alive instead of worshipping the ashes, meaning that traditions are never fixed. They are fluid and are always evolving and adapting.

Moreover, tradition is a very good way of being able to map changes in where things have come from and where they are now, because living traditions are able to grow, change, adapt, and evolve. That dichotomy is no longer seen as being such a stark thing, as "the modern is not the traditional and the traditional is not the modern". To put it very plainly, the modern and the traditional are actually one and the same.

Twenty years ago, when INTBAU was founded, professional discourse created a climate where "traditionalists" and "modernists" (even if they did not define themselves as such) were at odds with one another, and where anyone who wanted to design or to build in styles or with methods that were "traditional" was seen as totally backwards-looking or anti-progressive.

Fortunately, there's much more of a middle ground now. Architecture and conversations on style have in many cases become more pluralised, and the environmental agenda has come to the fore, meaning that more people and practitioners realise there need to be different and better ways of building.

Traditional methods continue to exist, or have been revived and taught and disseminated, in rural areas. But within cities, the story can be different. Cities are dense conglomerations of people who are drawn there by the promise of better jobs, better prospects or, in fact, because they had no choice. But, as far as traditions are concerned, there you face numerous issues of land ownership, tenure, and the need to build more densely.

So, it's both interesting and complicated to think about the "modern" vs "traditional" dichotomy in the city context because cities bring people together in one place from all manner of other places, and thus having different priorities and perspectives, different ways of living, and different levels of availability of building materials. Thus, a question arises about which traditions should be kept alive and how exactly should they be adapted and evolved to suit an urban context. There's no question that that's possible... it's just what needs to be in place to help it happen – rather than what is happening now in cities around the world, when we see concrete assembled quickly into unsafe, unmaintainable high-rises, constructed to accommodate a fast-growing urban population.

F: The global construction industry accounts for 25 to 40 percent of the world's total carbon emissions and I know that one of the practical reasons to support traditional and indigenous architecture is sustainability. Since 2001, your institution has initiated dozens of workshops and research projects – could you highlight some of the techniques, methods, or systems of knowledge that best describe traditional architecture's potential in terms of making architecture and local economies sustainable?

H: I can give three examples from different parts of the world and the first one will be Pakistan. For the last three or so years we've been working with Yasmeen Lari on something she calls "barefoot architecture". As a part of this project, we are working with people locally, organising training programmes to use certain traditional materials to build accommodation, outdoor cooking stoves, hand water pumps, eco-toilets, etc.

We also now have an INTBAU Training Centre as part of a Lari-designed campus at Makli, around 60 kilometres east of Karachi. Alongside the training centre are twenty-five residential guestroom accommodations, which means that people from villages locally can come to that site to join workshops. For example, they can learn to create bamboo panels and earth-lime mixes used in building, to do thatching with reeds and bamboo frames for roofs, to make outdoor cooking stoves, etc. After completing this training, they can take learnings back to their villages, where houses and shelters are often inadequate and unsafe in a region prone to floods and earthquakes.

Another example I'd like to give is related to deserts in the south of Morocco, known for its traditional earthen structures used by the locals. However, despite the fact that now around 30 percent of the world's population live in earth structures, the natural materials they are made of are widely associated with the past – and to that kind of "modern" vs "traditional" dichotomy we were speaking about at the beginning. Many people, understandably, do not want to build earthen structures because they are implicitly associated with the past, with poverty, or with a sort of "stuck" and backwards way of life, which results in an increasing number of houses made of "modern" and widely available concrete blocks. Concrete block houses don't perform well in the Moroccan climate. In the heat, they can become almost uninhabitably warm.

In partnership with Terrachidia, our chapter in Spain has been trying to help revive traditional methods and show that they are not of the past, but rather the embodiment of an extraordinary inheritance of wisdom and knowledge that's still really good and useful now. The work in Morocco is similar to that in Pakistan – finding masters that still continue working with local and natural materials, we invite people locally and internationally to come and learn by doing, through training sessions and workshops.

I'd also like to mention Sweden where, for the last few years, an annual summer school has been running – with an angle on classical architecture. It might sound like a really specific thing that's not going to be

relevant for the world's population, but the way we've chosen to plan the programme means that's not the case. Our summer school gives architecture students from all over the world a grounding in what a lot of them – no matter what programme they are coming from or where – feel is lacking in their architectural education: drawing, getting to know existing buildings in local and traditional styles adapted to climate and context, getting to observe them, and doing everything from measured drawing to urban planning (always with an exercise based on a real place locally). For these exercises we select places based on and informed by the needs of local communities that are concerned about recent or planned developments. Students and tutors on the summer school find ways of proposing reasonably simple changes, such as to street layout or to rework the facades of certain buildings, to help transform the place in terms of its feel and accessibility to citizens and visitors.

F: You've been managing this organisation for more than ten years: could you describe what you have learned and unlearned during this work? Do you have established internal mechanisms at INTBAU that allow your organisation to evolve and make your work more impactful?

H: The fact that the environmental agenda has increasingly come to the forefront in built environment discourse has helped me and INTBAU's own agenda enormously. Twenty years ago, the style wars between "traditionalists" and "modernists" were in full swing. And now, as you've rightly put

it in your question, there is widespread awareness that up to 40 percent of carbon emissions can be controlled by the full life cycle of a building. That's a huge challenge but also a huge opportunity for built environment industries to do something. And no one is saying that traditional methods are the only way. Of course, there'll be new methods and materials that we don't even yet know. But that said, there is the need to make sure that the traditional knowledge, the inherited, the indigenous, the vernacular, the local, have a seat at the table because certainly they all have something to contribute.

And what have I learned? To answer this question, we'd need hours, but I think that the nicest thing has been the network and the people that were initially running our seven chapters and that so far has grown into more than thirty. I see the collection of individuals and their commitment and the variety of everything they do – from an academic in Poland who is doing really essential research into the energy efficiency of heritage buildings, to the projects in Morocco, Pakistan and elsewhere that are making effective, tangible use of natural and replenishable materials to show how project life cycles can be better for people and the planet.

Creating Spaces for Islamic Art

Alaloui Ouajid Moulay Said is the founder of the Grand Musée de Marrakech and an esteemed member of the Majlis Honorary Committee. A native of Marrakech, he is a trained architect and a graduate of the École Spéciale d'Architecture in Paris. He has lived in Dubai, the USA, and France, but returned home to complete the founding and construction of the museum. He discusses broader notions of Islamic art and its curation and exhibition practices, as well as the role that traditional architecture can play in contemporary constructions.

Creating Spaces for Islamic Art

Grand Musée de Marrakech
Marrakech, Morocco

The Majlis: A Meeting Place   Architecture

BEN WHEELER:

In your mind, what value do collections of Islamic art hold – for nations and cities, but also for communities and individuals?

ALALOUI OUAJID
MOULAY SAID:

There is an essential aspect of Islamic art: everything is made for a purpose. This is a legacy of Islamic philosophy, reflected in material objects – a heritage we need to pass down to younger generations. For example, at one point in time we used to use candles to give light to a space and later learned to use electricity. But if we ever lose electricity, the past is there, we can always return to it. The knowledge of the past is always being adapted to the needs of the contemporary context. These collections underline and illuminate those links, emphasising the value they have for all. They have a beginning but no end.

B: Do you see any issues with how Islamic art is being exhibited globally?

A: It's important that we recognise the different types of exhibitions that are possible. Nowadays, curators often choose the best pieces that were owned by historically wealthy figures in power, such as emirs and sultans – and this is useful, because it preserves the knowledge of that period, these gifts from weddings or for special occasions, they show the highest level of creation during that period. This is what is exhibited most often in these museums and collections – but this is only part of Islamic art!

You have to focus on simple objects from the home, materials from everyday life – all these objects together make up Islamic art. We need to pair these collections with the right explanations of their historical and cultural contexts and functions, so that people don't get a skewed impression of the tradition. We need to teach this better, we need to encourage further research that moves beyond the surface level of this material, and this is what will improve the current state of exhibitions of Islamic art.

B: What do you believe are some of the essential principles of traditional architecture, and how were they implemented during the construction of the Grand Musée de Marrakech? Why are these techniques and materials important?

A: The museum, if you are to see it and experience it, answers these questions itself in a way. I am from Marrakech and the material surrounding my city made a large impact on its construction. There is very strong earth and the people there were really smart – they didn't need to go hundreds of kilometres away to collect stone, they used what they had: water and earth. You could even build a house on the same plot of land where you collected the earth! We followed this same philosophy with the museum, everything was made and done by hand, working with traditional techniques and paying homage not only to these practices, but to the materials that the land provided us with.

Craft

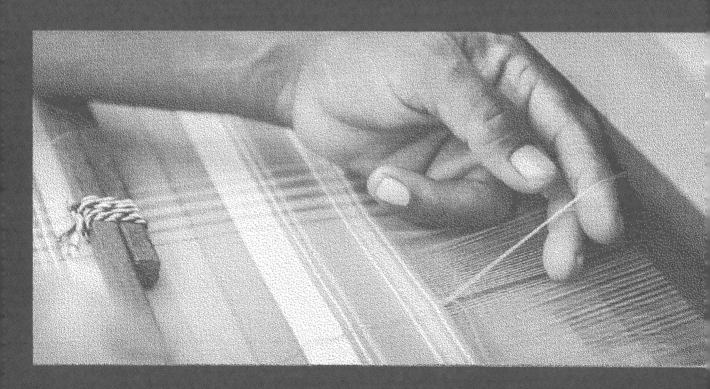

The Majlis is a celebration of craft. The hard work, the countless hours, and the passed-down forms of traditional knowledge that were a critical part of its conception and construction represent the inherent value of craft – not just for individuals, but for entire communities. This meeting of Colombia and Morocco, of bamboo and textile, assembled by Venetian craftspeople, illustrates how craft and the network surrounding it poses a potential answer to the question of "how will we live together?"

Sustainable and economically viable forms of craft practices are essential to the continued existence of local communities. The shared knowledge across these localities, be it knowledge of techniques, of materials, or of commercial strategies, aids in their continued growth. Craft is essential in that it provides a livelihood for many, but also because of the important role it plays in the expression of individual and collective identities. Craft is how a people show who they are to themselves and others. The Majlis celebrates both the history and future potential of craft as an individual and collective practice, as a form of heritage, and as a path leading us forward.

The Atlas
Weavers

The Majlis: A Meeting Place   Craft

The Majlis emphasises the value of preserving and empowering North-African craft practice in today's challenging market. In 2019, the team of Caravane Earth began working with the Ain Leuh Women's Cooperative in the Atlas Mountains of Morocco. As we worked to design and produce the central carpet for the Majlis, we developed an admiration for these brave women, who work against all odds with smiles on their dignified faces.

The slow process and formidable quality in their craft is steeped in regional traditions and geographical surroundings. They carry deep knowledge in natural dyeing, yarn spinning, and traditional weaving – all in their Beni Mguild kilim style. However, because younger generations see no perspective or financial stability in this knowledge, there is a chance these women will be the last who practise this astounding craft.

Weaving is an invaluable link in a chain of production practices that bind members of the community to each other and nature. Farmers, shepherds, spinners, dyers, weavers, and traders are all part of the process. Through teaching language and business skills and facilitating collaboration with designers on an international level, Caravane Earth plans to empower an ethical production of authentic Moroccan craft in today's market. Currently there are twenty-four active members of the Ain Leuh Women's Cooperative.

Above the Ain Leuh natural spring in the Atlas Mountains sits a village of just over 5,000 people. In 1977, local women formed a cooperative which has since sustained itself with minimal support, income, and exposure. The craft of weaving is an invaluable link in a complex chain of ancient cultural practices that bind a community. Farmers, herdsmen grazing the sheep, yarn makers, families, and merchants trading in the local souks all play their part in the process. Currently the members of the Ain Leuh Women's Cooperative represent many ages and abilities, as they integrate weaving into their daily lives and household duties. They love what they do and we love what they do.

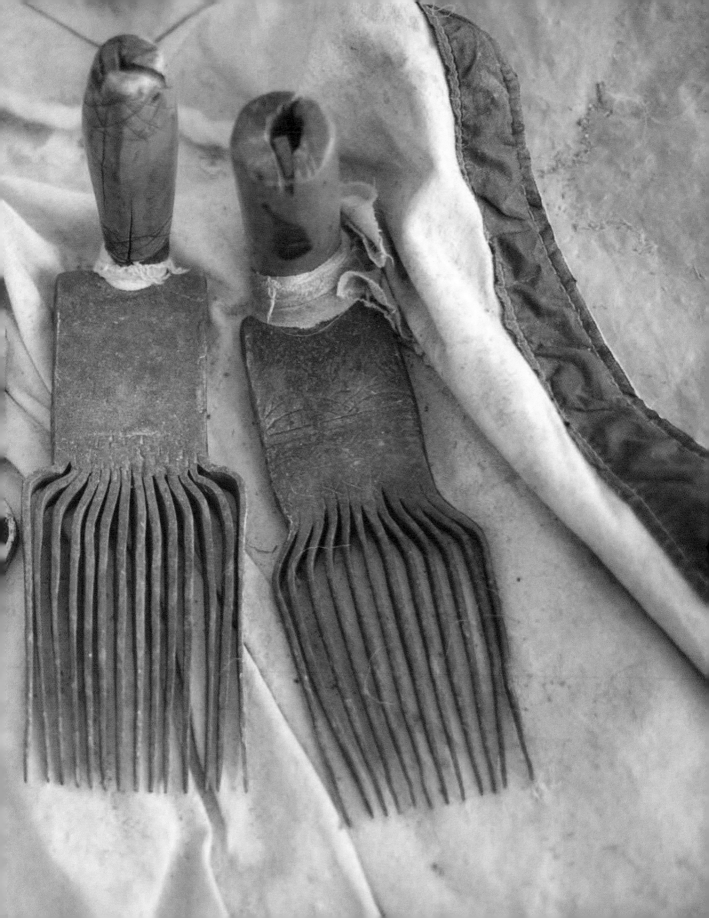

Prerna Saraaf and Nina Mohammad Galbert led the first Caravane Earth collaboration with Ain Leuh in making the centrepiece of the Majlis: a magnific carpet around which we will gather at the Venice Biennale with international groups of scholars, diplomats, storytellers, and guests to discuss how we will live together.

Working in their studio, we saw how hard this small group works to carry on the Beni Mguild kilim craft tradition. We saw how eager they were to teach others the geometric patterns and knotting techniques. We witnessed how sourcing, cleaning, spinning, weaving, knotting, combing, finishing, washing, and drying the wool – this intricate and specialised set of skills – is rewarded with as little as two dollars per day, deeming the practice economically obsolete. Artisanship in the community is constantly threatened by standard market prices determined by industrialised mass production. The overwhelming market of rugs dyed and cleaned with chemicals, woven to fast standards, and sold by middlemen provides a constant threat to North African heritage that goes back hundreds, sometimes thousands, of years.

Today, having grown up watching their parents in economic turmoil, young people often depart the mountains with hope for a better life in the cities. They leave the security of their cultural identity behind them, and in many cases continue to live in abject poverty. Caravane Earth recognises the need to stimulate and support local interest and personal investment in craft heritage. We recognise great value in the authenticity of techniques taught from loom to loom and handed down from generation to generation.

The Majlis: A Meeting Place   Craft

Making Artisan Voices Heard

Nina Mohammad-Galbert is the Creative Director at the Artisan Project, a pioneering sustainable sourcing and ethical design and craft production company, which was founded in Fès in 2011 and is now based in Tangier, Morocco. For the Majlis exhibition, she collaborated with three women – Khadaouj Ouchkek, Hachmia El Douiri, and Khadija El Aabdi – all from the Ain Leuh Women's Weaving Cooperative in Morocco, to create a collection titled "The Story of Yan". She discusses the contemporary state of the Moroccan carpet industry, some of the challenges facing the tradition, and some misconceptions about the authenticity of the craft.

BEN WHEELER:

Through your work, you speak about the lack of representation and the near invisibility of craftswomen – what do you think are some of the underlying reasons for the current conditions, and what are some potential ways to solve these issues?

NINA MOHAMMAD-GALBERT:

Looking at the history of the tradition, women were primarily making these carpets as part of a family unit, along with a variety of other household activities. Weaving was a tradition that was passed down from mother to daughter, and the creation of a household carpet, as well as other forms of textiles, was a labour of love rather than an economical obligation. During the French colonial period and the resulting industrialisation of carpet making, the Moroccan carpet became a valuable commodity and the female weavers became part of a very large supply chain, dominated and controlled by men who manage the industry and set the prices for the carpets, including the payment of the weavers. The carpet sellers tell a romantic story of how the carpets are traditionally made by women in the mountains, but when you go to the mountains you see that most of the women are living in poverty; not only are they invisible, they're also impoverished. Part of the challenge with most women's carpet co-operatives is that they don't have any way of reaching the consumers directly in order to make their voices heard and to engage with clients, and these sellers would like to keep it that way, as it allows them to alter prices

after production and to control most of the process. Due to the lack of language and social media skills, the women weavers rely on potential buyers finding them through poorly marketed local craft fairs and their cooperatives. Most cooperatives are difficult to find and rarely visited by Moroccan tourist guides and their clients. We at the Artisan Project understand that the key for sustainable economic growth for female-led cooperatives is to support both foreign-language education (primarily English) and social media skills – it's necessary to give these women the means to communicate directly, and in doing so they can potentially cut out the dealers and middlemen who are taking advantage of them, and target potential consumers directly.

B: What is the current state of the carpet-making tradition and how is it being passed down?

N: I think that, given the sheer amount of carpets that are made and sold, one might be surprised to find that, partially due to the conditions I described above, most of these women are not encouraging the next generation to practise this craft. The tradition is not being passed down because overall it is not a sustainable one. We can support vocational programmes, but only if the girls are truly committed and they see this is a tradition that they want to carry on. Given the contemporary state of the craft and the industry, it has to be made clear that these collectives, for example, can offer other skills – how to use a PC, language education, how to use social media, etc. Then they'll want to go there and be a part of it. "Saving"

the tradition isn't simply about encouraging young women to start making carpets – it's about providing an environment in which the craft actually benefits them in ways both educational and financial.

B: As a creative director, you most likely deal with subjective terms like "authentic" and "traditional" in regard to works of craft/art – in your mind, what makes a carpet either authentic or traditional, and what are maybe some of the misconceptions surrounding this terminology?

N: The easiest way to spot a "vintage" carpet is through its imperfections. If you think of the practice in context, a carpet may have quite an abstract design and you wonder why the maker weaved this diamond shape so imperfectly, but it may turn out she had to leave the carpet to do some other work, or she ran out of a particular colour. The physical evidence, the ability to track the tradition, is also fleeting – these objects are made from wool and are perishable. The carpets and their trends also reflect an ongoing history of exchange between a variety of actors. Many French designers, for instance, were actually bringing specific plans for the carpet makers to weave, and the women gradually started to incorporate some of these designs into other work. Today, many of the contemporary carpets are being designed prior to the weaving process, and therefore the weavers

are not using the traditional patterns that have been part of their ancestral heritage – only the knotting and weaving technique is authentic in this case. Having said that, the weavers I work with are not concerned with working only with traditional patterns or colours. Rather, they simply appreciate that a skill that they have honed and placed value in is being honoured.

Colombian Workers on Bamboo Cultivation

In interviews with members of the team of Simón Vélez and Marcelo Villegas, workers describe their relationships with guadua, a particularly large and flexible form of bamboo that is indigenous to Colombia. The same workers are responsible for the cultivation and construction of the guadua used to build the frame of the Majlis.

JOSÉ ANÍBAL OCHOA
carpenter

I have been a carpenter by profession for many years now. I started working with guadua about fifteen or twenty years ago, when I was studying at the technological university and had the opportunity to learn about the material through the help of Mr Simón Vélez and Mr Marcelo Villegas. They are the ones who pushed me to get to the point where I am today. At the time we knew guadua as a normal product that was simply used for making fences and normal forms of construction. Through this education I was able to learn more about it and I became excited. To me, it's a novelty. Even though it's one of the oldest elements, we didn't really know what it was capable of. Now, working with it and seeing its potential has been a very exciting experience for me.

ALONSO CÁRDENAS
civil engineer, carpenter

I've been a carpenter for a long time and I'm also a civil engineer. For over twenty years, I've been working with Simón Vélez on his guadua project and on all of his projects in general. After some experiences working in different areas of the world, I could see that people were often surprised by the beauty of this material. It made me think, "people are starting to learn about this material and are surprised by it, so how come we don't value it as much as we should?"

Whether we like it or not, guadua is an example of what the future holds for forests. As guadua grows, on average, about 10 centimetres a day, it produces more oxygen and it contributes to many things. Given the current rate of deforestation on our planet, in the near future we won't have the same capacity for wood consumption. Things are really heading that way.

JAVIER CASTAÑO
carpenter

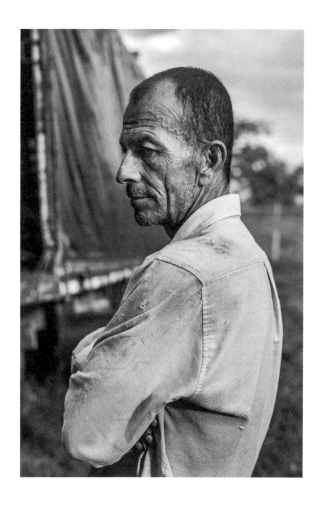

Basically, all of my brothers are involved in this work; I also have a son who also works with guadua. I have cousins, brothers, nephews, and uncles that work with guadua. It's like a chain – in my extended family there are between thirty and forty members working with guadua. My day starts at 7.00 a.m. and I work until 4.00 p.m., but often I work until 8.00 p.m. when the trucks arrive late. In those cases, I have to make an extra effort and work until that time to take care of the trucks. The hardest part of my job is the winter-

time, because guadua gets too wet and as a result it becomes too straight. Guadua is dangerous when you are on an incline. You have to know how to handle it and to do so with lots of care. I've been practising this trade for thirty-five years. My father actually taught me all about guadua. He passed away nine years ago but today his children are still here and we represent him. I am very grateful because this is my family's sustenance and that is not only true for me, it's true for many.

Assembling the Majlis

The design and construction of the Majlis included international cooperation between teams in Colombia and Morocco. In keeping with the themes of community and collaboration, this diverse team of craftspeople was meant to meet in person in Venice to share the experience of raising the Majlis. Due to the Covid-19 pandemic, this was simply not possible. Instead, the Majlis team was expanded to include local Venetian weavers and carpenters, who were then in communication with the rest of this wide network and completed the final process of assembling the special structure. These less-than-ideal circumstances resulted in a positive solution: to grow the knowledge and community surrounding the Majlis.

Living with the Art of Craft

In the world of furniture making and interior design, the Earl of Snowdon is known as David Linley. A great connoisseur of craftsmanship and supporter of sustainable solutions for living spaces, he joined the Majlis as a member of its Honorary Committee. Here, Lord Snowdon speaks about his approach, the main values of his work, and the future of housing.

Living with the Art of Craft

LESIA PROKOPENKO:

What does work with living spaces mean to you? And what does this process consist of?

DAVID LINLEY:

Normally I try to start with a blank canvas. One of the most important things is to understand the proportions of the living space, be it a kitchen, a drawing room, or a study. In assessing the proportions, you should consider the light, the way you move around the space, in and out of it. I would start by looking at the corners, deciding what I need to put in the architrave or window surrounds; whether you want the room to be light or dark. For example, if you are in a study, you need to be able to draw or to read there. And I need to think of a focal point in the room: whether to have a fireplace or what kind of treatment there is on the floor. These are the considerations to start with. And then I build up layers. It's a traditional approach, much like in painting and sculpture: whether the interior needs to resonate with views of the landscape outside the window and similar aspects like that. Two key things here are practicality and comfort; I don't like overtly grand spaces. I do like big open spaces and clean lines, but I also like places where you can relax and be comfortable. I love music, so how the speakers are positioned is important. Sitting at a dining table or a desk, you need to know what kind of chairs are comfortable. They can be multipurpose, but if you have to sit for a long time, you wouldn't want to use dining chairs. There should be a combina-

tion of different chairs, including ones that are good for your back. I covered my office chairs in linen to make them look nice, but in sitting for hours on end in front of the computer, the chairs didn't like it: they were meant for dining and just short periods of sitting on. We also have to think about the surfaces within the living space: whether you place any photographs there, memories of your childhood, of your children. These can instantly give you comfort.

L: Where does your passion for interior design come from? How did you start working with it?

D: People who make furniture and design spaces are also sculptors. I suppose what intrigued me about that came from my interest in engineering and how you make something – the practicality of it, how you use it. The choice of materials always matters. I like working with wood, a material that looks nicer with age. It's always my aim to combine the two elements of practicality and comfort, and to feel that you're making something for the long term. I always encourage people to collect wood because it's a beautiful material: slow growing and natural; we should cherish it. There are different ways to be inspired, sometimes from the pleasure of the very tools the maker uses. This gets lost when people are designing things for a machine to make: you have no real concern for the person making it.

L: And what are the origins of your appreciation for craft? Why is craftsmanship important today?

D: Craft is a beautiful word, but a complicated one too, it can mean so many things. Children at school are told, "Now you've got some time, you can go and do some arts and crafts". Some may consider it a sort of thing that doesn't really matter. But I think craft has greater resonance now, people are looking for something that is man-made, that has the impact of a human rather than a machine. And it's not just about making: it's related to philosophy and psychology. It has so much to do with art.

L: What are your main values when it comes to designing interiors and furniture?

D: When I started, there were so many people who would say to my mother, "He's still going to get a proper job!" And a lot of my role is actually showing that it is a proper job: it's a way of life, a very nice and calm practice compared to the work that makes people burned out. Many try to find pleasure in their work but all they do is sit at their computer. They may be successful, they can make money, but what is it that they leave behind in the world? History is learned from objects and the way things were made, from ancient Roman coins to Stonehenge – the way it was made is still a mystery! Craft does have this wonderful mystery around it, an aura that people are wanting more and more of nowadays.

L: How do you envision the future of people's homes?

D: We see people's homes growing more efficient. With climate change, there is interest in insulation, and also in ventilation since Covid. I think that's a very curious conundrum. We require buildings cleverly designed to capture solar and wind energy, and there should be new solutions for dealing with waste, and the wastage of water: perhaps tanks for collecting water. There are so many things to consider in terms of design and the materials we'll be using in the future. For example, whether these materials are sensibly resourced; what's amazing is we have so many options to experiment with. The materials of old could be re-energised, for example, wool could be weaved with something more durable. There's a lot of thought going into these aspects at the moment and how to work in ways that benefit the environment.

L: Is there any dream project you'd like to accomplish?

D: I'm always looking forward to new work. There are people whom I admire that I'd love to do a project with, to think with them in a different way. I've been very lucky to work with great architects and designers. I'm not an actual designer, I'm the one who puts makers and designers together – to get that lovely combination, like we said before, of art and craft.

The Multifaceted
World of Craft

The Smithsonian Institution Center for Folklife and Cultural Heritage has been an essential organisation in supporting and preserving vital craft practices around the globe. Marjorie Hunt, a folklife curator and education specialist with the Institution, will take part in the Majlis symposium in October 2021, which features round-table discussions with important global figures from the worlds of architecture and craft, film screening, and demonstrations from craftspeople. Here she discusses the challenges and success stories of those that have managed to keep craft alive.

BEN WHEELER:

Within the scope of arts and culture, do you feel like there has been an increased interest in craft as a topic of discussion?

MARJORIE HUNT:

My experience has been mainly with craftspeople in the United States. There's such a rich array of traditional crafts being practised in different regional and cultural communities across the country that it's very difficult to generalise, but I think on the whole there has been a marked increase in interest and appreciation for traditional craft in the U.S. over the past several decades. In the case of Native American basketry, many of these centuries-old traditions were in decline in the mid-1900s, with only a few practitioners left. While they still face daunting challenges, including the loss of elders and their specialised knowledge, dwindling or inaccessible natural resources, and the profusion of cheap mass-produced goods, many Native basketry traditions have experienced a resurgence in recent years due in large part to the resilience and creativity of tribal members dedicated to preserving and passing on their cultural heritage to younger generations within their communities, and efforts to increase the public's understanding and recognition of the beauty, value, and meaning of Native baskets as art forms that are rooted in community life and deeply connected to the local environment. One of the most important developments has been the formation of Native basket weaving organisations that have been active in teaching, promoting, getting young people interested, and educating the broader public. A great example is the Maine Indian Basketmakers Alliance (MIBA), which is made up of basket weavers from the four Wabanaki Indian tribes in Maine – the Maliseet, Micmac, Passamaquoddy, and Penobscot. Since its founding in 1993, MIBA has revitalised the ash and sweet-grass basketry tradition of Wabanaki people, lowering the average age of basket makers from sixty-three to forty, and increasing the number of basket weavers in the region from fifty-five to more than 200, spanning four generations. More and more young people are actively involved, finding a renewed sense of pride in their tribal identity and heritage through basket making. More broadly speaking, I think that as a society we've moved so far in the direction of mechanisation, mass production, and the digital world that we're increasingly seeing a desire for the humanity of the handmade, for the connection to human skill, knowledge, and values that handcrafted work embodies.

B: What are some ways in which communities can structure the sales of local craft while still maintaining a tangible record of these cultural artefacts? In your experience, are there practices of archiving the end result of craft so that some record stays within the community, or does the exchange of goods for money create problems for their preservation?

M: We work collaboratively with communities to document their craft traditions. We conduct interviews with artisans; take photographs of tools, techniques, and steps in the process; make videos; and document completed works. These materials are deposited in our archives, where they are widely accessible to the general public and to the communities themselves. Very importantly, we readily make copies of this documentation available to the tradition-bearers we work with through our Shared Stewardship policy. And we work closely with community members to aid them in documenting their own cultural expressions. In many cases, it is the craftspeople themselves who are leading the way in researching and revitalising craft traditions and techniques. The late Teri Rofkar, a Tlingit weaver and basket maker from Alaska, conducted meticulous research in museum collections and spent countless hours figuring out how to weave the once-lost art of the ancient Raven's Tail robe. Thanks to her tireless efforts, and the work of several other talented weavers, the Raven's Tail robe is once again dancing in Alaska Native communities. There's been an exciting shift in museum practice. Many museums recognise the fact that traditional practitioners are cultural authorities, experts in their art forms and traditional ways of life, and they are welcomed into the collections; there's a strong commitment to supporting community members in their efforts to conduct research, document their traditions, and share their knowledge.

Master Tlingit weaver and basket maker Teri Rofkar from Sitka, Alaska, worked to research and revive the once-lost art of weaving the ancient Raven's Tail robe. Photo by Tom Pich Photography/NYC

Third-generation potter Vernon Owens in his workshop at Jugtown Pottery in Seagrove, North Carolina. Photo by Tom Pich Photography/NYC

B: In instances where a tradition has become obsolete due to changing circumstances, should the practice still be encouraged? If so, how? How do we account for crafts that may still be seen as essential to cultural identities but are no longer economically/practically viable?

M: There are some great success stories in communities in the United States. One in particular is the southern stoneware pottery tradition, which has been practised continuously for more than 200 years in North Carolina, northern Georgia, and parts of Alabama – areas rich in local clay deposits. The early potters crafted utilitarian wares for their farming neighbours – churns, jugs, jars, and milk crocks – so that they could make butter and preserve their home-grown fruits, vegetables, and meats. When glass, metal, and plastic containers came into widespread use, there was little demand for the potters' skills and the tradition fell into decline. Many of the old family shops closed, but some of the potteries adapted to the new situation and reinterpreted their traditional craft; they pivoted to meet the demands of a new market outside their community. Potters started making new forms, such as coffee mugs and tea pots, that appealed to the tourist market, as well as older forms and fine pieces valued by collectors; and they adopted a broader range of glaze colours. But they continue to find inspiration in the old pottery tradition and to care deeply about their local heritage. They still insist on digging and preparing their own local clay and firing their wares in wood-fired kilns, making beautifully-crafted pots that are a creative blend of tradition and innovation. Today, this 200-year-old art form is flourishing in the American South, evidence of a dynamic, evolving tradition.

Earth

The earth serves as both a literal and symbolic foundation for the Majlis. The structure's composite parts, grown from the soil and woven from the wool of sheep who graze on the land, are surrounded by a garden planned and planted to evoke a connection to local flora and provide for the residents of the abbey for years to come. Caravane Earth, through multiple initiatives, including the Majlis and the organisation's working farm in Doha, Heenat Salma, continues to engage directly with issues concerning the earth and its treatment. There are many themes that are highlighted by the Majlis: bringing together craftspeople who are working with sustainable practices, and making positive systemic impact in social, cultural, and ecological realms, which all come down to a greater appreciation and understanding of the earth, of soil, of the shared ground beneath all of our feet.

The Majlis
Garden

The Majlis: A Meeting Place   Earth

Todd Longstaffe-Gowan is an internationally-renowned landscape architect who has worked on a number of historic landscapes, including The Tower of London, Hampton Court Palace, Kensington Palace Gardens, and The Crown Estate (Central London). He conceived and designed the garden at Abbazia di San Giorgio Maggiore, which serves as an accompaniment to the Majlis exhibition. He discusses the many historical and cultural considerations that went into the planning stages of the project, and provides his thoughts on the real role and function of public gardens.

BEN WHEELER:

To start off, could you give us a short introduction to your part in the Majlis project?

TODD LONGSTAFFE-GOWAN:

I was invited to join the project by the exhibition curator Dr Thierry Morel, and was involved from early 2020 in trying to find a suitable site for the Majlis. It wanted to be large and airy as we were determined that Simón Vélez and Stefana Simic's extraordinary bamboo building should sit in a garden, and that this outdoor space, like the Majlis itself, should provide a setting for, and promote, social interaction and community cohesion – aims which echoed those of the curator of the 17th International Architectural Exhibition, Hashim Sarkis, who encouraged participants "to imagine spaces in which we can generously live together". Having investigated several potential sites for the Majlis, we agreed that the garden of the Abbazia di San Giorgio Maggiore was perfectly suited for the project. Lying a stone's throw from the Doge's Palace and Piazza San Marco, the historic and very architecturally distinguished monastic establishment was centrally placed and readily accessible by vaporetto, and it possessed a large, sunny and unelaborated garden. We are grateful to Carmelo Grasso, Director of the Abbazia di San Giorgio Benedicti Claustra Onlus, the Abbot Emeritus, and the Benedictine community for embracing enthusiastically our proposals. The monastic setting had a significant impact on the evolving design of what was to become

the Majlis garden. San Giorgio was established in 982 AD by the Benedictine monk Giovanni Morosini, and is known to have had extensive productive gardens that were documented in generalised topographical views during the 16th and 17th centuries. We know surprisingly little about the detail of these gardens, but we can be reasonably certain that they were productive, and that the monks cultivated a great range of fruit, vegetables, and culinary and medicinal herbs. Venice was the centre of the medieval European spice and exotic plant trade. The Republic's monopoly on the importation and redistribution of exotic spices and plants for medicinal, culinary, commercial, and ornamental purposes bolstered the so-called "Myth of Venice" by emphasising its power, unlimited magnificence, and its access to foreign resources and the luxury trades. The gardens of its monastic institutions were among the Veneto's earliest botanical laboratories, and their flora rich and varied.

B: You're involved in so many different projects, both public and private, in different parts of the world. What do you think is particularly unique about this one?

T: Although I've made many ephemeral gardens in my day, the garden we're proposing to build on San Giorgio shall be different: it's designed for an exhibition, but shall have an afterlife. It is in this regard a very sustainable project. Although I find the evanescence of temporary oases very alluring, I wish to create something more lasting and hopefully more productive. I furthermore wish to make something distinctive to the gardens one commonly sees in Venice – something that evokes an earlier, more lively, and exuberant gardening tradition. As I have said already, Venice was once at the forefront of gardening and botanical experimentation, and the Republic's monastic gardens were among its more fascinating laboratories. I believe therefore that our garden at San Giorgio presents a wonderful opportunity to create a living, working garden – full of fruit, flowers, and vegetables – that both evokes an historic tradition and addresses current ecological issues of sustainability.

B: What about this specific location? Obviously, you studied its history and its role in the history of the circulation of plants, materials, ideas, and flavours. How did that affect your curatorial choice?

T: San Giorgio, on the island of San Giorgio, is one of the most conspicuous and well-known landmarks in Venice; its soaring brick campanile rivals that of San Marco, and its 16th-century white marble façade is a masterpiece of the celebrated architect Andrea Palladio. Gardens have been cultivated on the island for well over a millennium, and the layouts of some of those dating from the early 16th century are documented in topographical views now in the city's Correr Museum. They are, of course, reasonably generalised – that is, the artists who recorded them were less interested in the accuracy of their representation than in conveying their presence. We do not, therefore – at least to my knowledge – have detailed records of the early garden layouts; and nor do we have detailed accounts of what was cultivated within them. In as much as we are keen to evoke rather than to recreate an early monastic garden, we have consulted one or two specialists. Isabella dalla Ragione – President of the Fondazione Archeologia Arborea and a leading light in the initiatives to preserve local (Italian) biodiversity and safeguarding traditional knowledge, rural culture, and oral history – has been particularly helpful and insightful. She has advised us on what plants would be most suitable for our garden and where we might find them in cultivation. Her list of recommended species has guided our final choice, and includes exotic (non-native) plants which were introduced to Veneto in the late Middle Ages and the Renaissance, as well as a range of vegetables and medicinal, culinary, and aromatic herbs which are locally distinctive to the Veneto – such as Cuban oregano (Plectranthus amboinicus), Erba di San Pietro (Tanacetum balsamita), Venetian varieties of artichokes (Cynara cardunculus var. Violetta di S. Erasmo and Precoce di Chioggia), or local varieties of summer cabbages (cavolfiore precoce, cavolo romanesco precoce, cavolo broccolo calabrese precoce, cavolo cappuccio precoce, and cavolo verza Estoril precoce).

B: What about this specific monastery? Did it have its own garden?

T: The Abbazia di San Giorgio used to have extensive productive and ornamental gardens. It now has only a small area immediately east of the church – about one third of an acre. This area was for many years a rather bleak hardstanding until about eleven years ago when it was converted, under the auspices of Mr Grasso, into four grass panels bisected by broad gravel paths. It is a large garden by Venetian standards. For several years the monks have kept chickens within a primitive coop and enclosure in one quadrant. All the chickens are named after famous Venetian artists: the cockerel is called Tintoretto after Jacopo Tintoretto, whose last work – *The Entombment of Christ* – was painted for the Benedictines' mortuary chapel in 1594.

B: You've mentioned in previous interviews that you value the element of surprise in your gardens. Don't give too much away, but what might surprise visitors to this space?

T: Yes, I'm reasonably certain that visitors will be surprised – perhaps not by the garden itself (though I hope it shall be visually striking), but by the fact that the monastery possesses one at all. The garden is not generally open to the public, and can only presently be seen by visitors who make their way to the top of the campanile – from which one gains a very good aerial prospect of the island and its surroundings, and indeed the whole of Venice.

B: A final and broad question: what should a public garden do? You've worked in so many diverse contexts, particularly with historic palace gardens, and this is obviously very different. But are there similarities?

T: A broad question indeed! First, I should make clear that although the Majlis garden shall be open for the duration of the Biennale (May till November 2021), it is not a public garden: it is a private garden with controlled public access. All gardens – from the most humble to the very grandest – should in my estimation be laid out with a view to creating beautiful spaces for recreation and enjoyment – whether communal, public, or private. They should be places where people can escape from the everyday world, whether they wish to commune with nature, read a book, or simply "zone out".

The Plants of the Majlis Garden

The garden designed by landscape architect Todd Longstaffe-Gowan establishes the environment of the Majlis and celebrates the pre-eminent role of Venice in introducing to Europe exotic flora from the Orient. With plants from Mediterranean regions that will thrive in the local climate for many years after the Majlis moves on, the garden creates a lasting legacy for the monastery of San Giorgio Maggiore; it will remain at the Abbazia as a gift to Venice from the Caravane Earth foundation.

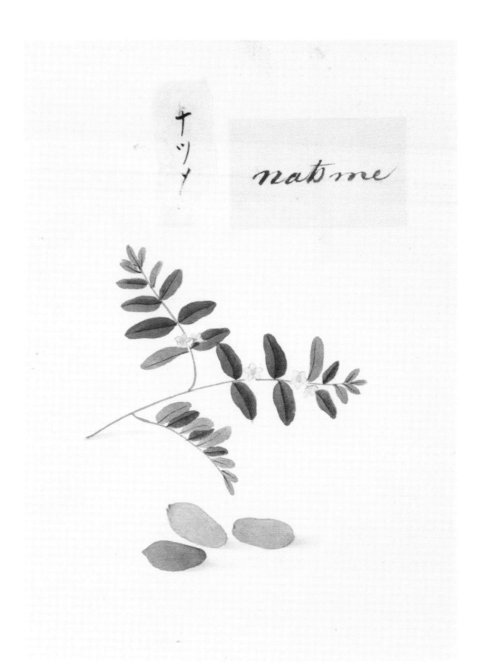

JUJUBE TREE
Ziziphus jujuba

The jujube – commonly known as the red or Chinese date – is among the most exotic introductions to Venice and one of the oldest cultivated fruit trees in the world. Known to Pliny and Ulysses, the medicinal and culinary fruit had certainly been introduced to the Veneto by the late 14th century. It was later included in Bartolomeo Scappi's *Opera* (1570; a collection of traditional Venetian recipes). The zízole tree was described by Frederic Eden in *A Garden in Venice* (1903) as "zigzaggy in its form" and "phonetically named".

POMEGRANATE
Punica granatum

GRENADIER SAUVAGE.

It is possible that the fruit was introduced to Venice from Persia at the time of Marco Polo. Textiles bearing pomegranate designs became popular in Venice in the 15th century, having been introduced from the Near East.

GINGER
Zingiber officinale

Credited with both preventative and curative properties, and valued for its pungent and spicy flavour, ginger has for many centuries been popular in the Veneto for cooking, drinking, and medicinal purposes. By the middle of the 15th century, several thousand tons of ginger and pepper were being imported to Venice annually.

HYSSOP
Hyssopus officinalis

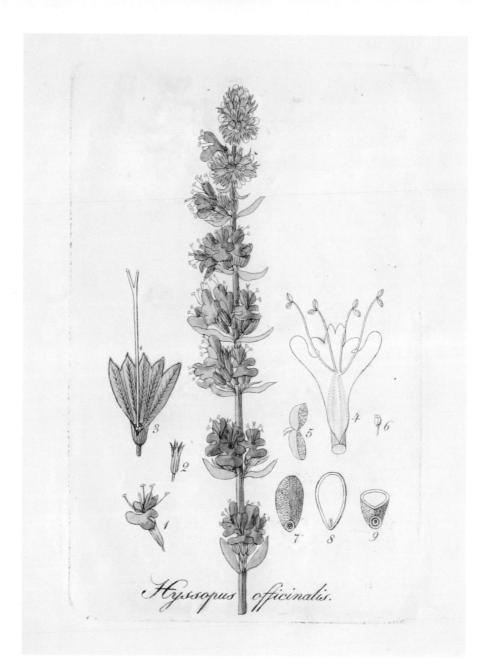

Hyssopus officinalis.

A common Mediterranean herb, hyssop was used in Venice in the celebration of the Marriage of the Sea (Sposalizio del Mare) – a ceremony established around 1,000 AD to symbolise the maritime dominion of Venice. After the prayer was completed, the Doge and his suite were aspersed, and the rest of the water was poured into the sea while the priests chanted the words "purge me with hyssop and I shall be clean" ("Aspérges me, Dómine, hyssópo et mundábor, Lavábis me, et super nivem dealbábor").

CUBAN OREGANO
Plectranthus amboinicus

Known variously as Cuban oregano, Mexican mint, and Indian borage, this semi-succulent and aromatic plant has been cultivated in the Veneto for many centuries. The herb was traditionally used for the treatment of respiratory and throat infections, as well as rheumatism, constipation, flatulence, and as an aid to stimulate lactation.

Heenat Salma: An Organic Farm in the Making

Heenat Salma, created by Caravane Earth, will include educational activities related to organic farming, traditional architecture, and crafts, but will also work to set internal standards and formulate values that will transform the whole locality. As the project moves forward, Heenat Salma will continue to signify a learning opportunity for both guests of the farm and Caravane Earth as an institution.

The Majlis: A Meeting Place   Earth

Heenat Salma

Heenat Salma is a farm in the village of Um El Qahab, located north of Doha, Qatar. The farm was founded by Caravane Earth as a hub for social transformation, affording peers the chance to build, learn, and interact beyond online experiences. Grounded in a dedication to agriculture, climate, and well-being, Heenat Salma is deeply concerned about the ongoing deterioration of all three.

The activities of the farm are our way of taking the helm, of steering initiatives towards a positive impact on humans globally and locally. Through tangible approaches, the farm functions as a prototype, as we examine and test new ways of enacting change. Heenat Salma is tackling pressing issues, such as the impact of the climate crisis on immigration influx, through a quest for sustainable solutions that lead to equitable relationships with farmers and craftspeople, both migrant and local, increased interconnectivity, and new forms of knowledge exchange.

Like most life on earth, the activities of Heenat Salma are concerned with and dependent on soil. Soil was an essential part of the founding of the farm. In 2019, Caravane Earth brought together a group of dedicated experts in agronomy, architecture, and water infrastructure to develop a holistic farm model and a ten-year strategy aimed at converting a conventional farm into a centre for regenerative agriculture that would be working in the extreme climatic conditions of the Arabian Peninsula. This was the beginning of Heenat Salma: an initiative in the form of a farm, dedicated to holistic methods in agriculture, architecture, and community development.

For soil to yield vital produce, it must first be alive. This stands in stark contrast to the extensive use of chemical fertilisers and the industrialisation of agriculture, which have led to land erosion and water scarcity, along with a worldwide loss of vitality, resilience, and nutritional value in the crops we eat. The holistic methods of Heenat Salma will offer an alternative model, allowing the farm to be fully sustained without the use of any chemicals. The farm will also practise simple techniques that bring animal waste, plant waste, and soil into a healthy relationship, transforming each element into fertility in the farm organism.

The farm's infrastructure is made up of a blend of hospitality and education. The direct sale of organic produce, its lodges, farm-to-table kitchen, concept store with hand picked objects produced by local and international craftspeople, its schedule of wellness and craft-oriented events: all are meant to serve as an engine that will support the whole project, its workers, and the further development and promotion of organic agriculture in the extreme conditions of the Arabian peninsula. The official launch of the farm is planned for 1 January 2022. We hope to see you at Heenat Salma soon.

Farming Almanacs of Filāḥa

Filāḥa is a lesser-known traditional agriculture technique that goes beyond more than just sustainability; it speaks to the beauty and ethics involved in sustaining the proper relationship between humans, plants, and the earth. Filāḥa has historical links to Andalucia but in fact pertains to a whole swathe of Muslim regions much wider than the Mediterranean, ranging from Morocco to Central Asia. Caravane Earth is currently incubating an educational programme related to Filāḥa as part of the activities of Heenat Salma farm that will encourage the study and implementation of these critical practices.

المزمن العارض بغرختي ولوجع الضنده ؏ ؏ ؏ ؏ ؏ ؏

صنعه الشراب الذي يقال له فيدس ؞؞

وهو شراب الزيت الرطب قد ينبغي ان يغسل الزيت بتاب ما المحزر وما
بعماحتي تنطف ويصير الما الذي يغسل به ما صافيا ثم يغسل بما عذب ولقي بعلى

كلما نابه كيران جوانس من العصير اوفيس من الزيت واذا ادراً وسكن
علانه بقال وخزن في الاوابي هذا الشراب لنخزن يضم ؞؞

صنعه شراب الافسنتين ؞؞

Folio from an Arabic version of *De materia medica* by Dioscorides.
Written and illustrated by Abdullah ibn al-Fadl. Iraq, 1224
F 1953.91 / Freer Gallery of Art

> "Husbandry is the foundation of civilisation – all sustenance derives from it, as well as the principal benefits and blessings that civilisation brings."

> Ibn ʿAbdūn in his treatise on Ḥisba, *c.* 1147, Seville

The Arabic words filāḥa, meaning "cultivation, tillage", and by extension "agriculture, farming, husbandry", and fallāḥ – "husbandman, tiller of the soil, peasant, farmer" – are derived from the verbal form falaḥa meaning "to cleave, split", and, in particular, "to plough, till, cultivate the land". It also means "to thrive, prosper, be successful, lucky, or happy", the two meanings being brought together beautifully by Ibn ʿAbdūn in the quotation above. Moreover, the word is sung out from the minarets of every mosque throughout the Muslim world five times each day during the call to prayer – hayya ʿala ʾl-falāḥ: "Come to success, come to salvation". Husbandry, well-being (in this world and the next) and worship are thus inextricably linked in the Arabic language.

This may come as some surprise. The Arabs, in popular imagination, came out of the desert as nomadic sheep- and camel-herders or breeders of fine horses, pastoralists rather than cultivators, and the Islamic civilisation they engendered and spread through half the world is renowned more for its accomplishments in urban architecture and the decorative arts, its learning in philosophy, mathematics, medicine and the sciences, and for its technical inventiveness and mercantile success than for any particular proficiency in agriculture. Yet, three thousand years before Islam, farmers in what is now Yemen were skilfully terracing rain-fed mountain slopes and cultivating wadis by means of spate irrigation to create what the ancient Greeks called Eudaimon Arabia, and the Romans Arabia Felix – "happy, fortunate, flourishing Arabia" – on account of its abundant fruits and flocks. Elsewhere, in Eastern Arabia, intensive oasis agriculture based on subterranean falāj irrigation was being developed as early as 1000 BCE. The Arabs already had a long history of farming when, with the spread of Islam from the 7th century AD, this expertise produced a remarkable resurgence in agriculture, especially in water harvesting and irrigation, in conjunction with the local knowledge of farmers in Iraq and Syria, Palestine and Jordan, Persia, Egypt, North Africa, Sicily, and Spain (each with their own long traditions of husbandry).

By the early 9th century most parts of the world under Islamic governance were experiencing an extension of agriculture into lands which had never been cultivated or which had long been abandoned. By means of newly introduced crops, the widespread diffusion of irrigation technology, and the more intensive rotations that these made possible, marked improvements were achieved in the productivity of agricultural land and labour. Over the next 500–700 years, with variations from place to place, agriculture thrived. In *The Mind of the Middle Ages*, the historian of ideas, Frederick B. Artz, writes: "The great Islamic cities of the Near East, North Africa and Spain [...] were supported by an elaborate agricultural system that included extensive irrigation and an expert knowledge of the most advanced agricultural methods in the world. The Muslims reared the finest horses and sheep and cultivated the best orchards and vegetable gardens. They knew how to fight insect pests, how to use fertilizers, and they were experts at grafting trees and crossing plants to produce new varieties." And Thomas Glick, writing of Muslim Spain, says: "Fields that had been yielding one crop yearly at most prior to the Muslims were now capable of yielding three or more crops in rotation [...] Agricultural production responded to the demands of an increasingly sophisticated and cosmopolitan urban population by providing the towns and cities with a variety of products unknown in Northern Europe." The flourishing, cultivated, predominantly urban civilisation of classical Islam was only made possible, and was largely dependent upon, an equally sophisticated and fertile revolution in the countryside.

Although the notion of a medieval Arab Agricultural Revolution, first proposed by Andrew Watson in 1974, or of an Islamic Green Revolution as called by others, has been challenged by some scholars, this is not the place to recapitulate the argument, which seems to revolve around matters of degree and detail rather than substance. What is clear is the marked change in the way farming was done, and its undoubted success. The new agriculture that followed in the wake of Islam and emerged across much of the Middle East and Mediterranean world appears to have

been quite different from the Roman, Byzantine, Sassanian, and Visigoth models that preceded it. It resulted from the synthesis of a number of new and old elements, skilfully worked into a productive and sustainable system, giving it a particular, characteristic stamp. The elements of the new agriculture, identified and meticulously documented by Watson in his seminal study on agricultural innovation in the early Islamic world, can be summarised in the following way.

Foremost was the introduction, acclimatisation, and further diffusion of new food crops, mainly fruit trees, grains, and vegetables, but also plants used for fibres, condiments, beverages, medicines, narcotics, poisons, dyes, perfumes, cosmetics, timber, and fodder, as well as garden flowers and ornamental plants. The most important of these new crops were sorghum, Asiatic rice, hard wheat, sugar cane, Old World cotton, and some citrus fruits, as well as such exotics as the banana and plantain, coconut, watermelon, mango, spinach, Colocasia, globe artichoke, and aubergine. The influx of new crops and plants, many of which came from India, South-East Asia and Central Africa, was only made possible by the unprecedented unification of a large part of the Old World under Islam, which facilitated long-distance travel by merchants, diplomats, scholars, and pilgrims, and unleashed the free movement of peoples from very different climates and agricultural traditions – Indians, Malays, Persians, Yemenis, Africans, Berbers, and Syrians, among others. This human flow and cultural exchange facilitated not only the diffusion of crops and plants but the knowledge of how to grow them. At the same time, a fertile intellectual climate of scientific enquiry and experimentation among botanists and agronomists, and the propensity of traditional husbandmen everywhere to select for local conditions, produced a profusion of cultivars of the old and new crops (as well as new breeds of livestock). For example, in the 9th century, Al-Jāḥiẓ stated that 360 kinds of dates were to be found in the market of Basra; in the early 10th century, Ibn Rusta reported 78 kinds of grapes in the vicinity of Sanaʿāʾ in Yemen; Al-Anṣārī, writing of a small town on the North African coast in about 1400, said that the environs produced 65 kinds of grapes, 36 kinds of pears, 28 kinds of figs, and 16 kinds of apricots; and in the 15th century, Al-Badrī wrote that in the region of Damascus 21 varieties of apricots, 50 varieties of raisins, and 6 kinds of roses were to be found. For the Yemen, Varisco records at least 88 named varieties of sorghum, the staple crop, documented in literary sources or used today in the field. The range of crops and plants grown (and eaten) was unparalleled.

The newly introduced crops induced significant changes in cultural methods. Because many of them originated in hot, moist, tropical and sub-tropical climates, in their new environment they needed the heat of summer, traditionally a "dead" season in Middle Eastern and Mediterranean agriculture which had hitherto been more or less restricted to crops that could be grown in the cooler but wetter winter months. Many of the new crops had to be irrigated, but the bonus of a new summer growing season led to the widespread adoption of systems of crop rotation and multiple cropping that allowed two, three, and even four crops

a year to be taken from the same piece of land, summer and winter, where before, in the Roman, Byzantine, and Judaic agricultural traditions, there had been at best one crop a year, and most commonly one every two years. Such intensive cropping regimes would inevitably deplete the soil of its natural fertility if not replenished, so the new farming redressed the balance with copious (though carefully controlled) applications of all kinds of organic manures, natural fertilizers, composts, mulches, and minerals, incidentally bringing about a closer integration between cultivation and the rearing of livestock.

While not all the new agriculture was dependent on artificial irrigation, many of the new crops – especially sugar cane and rice, and to a lesser degree cotton and some of the tropical and sub-tropical fruits – were water-hungry crops. The development of sophisticated systems for harvesting, storing, and distributing water was a hallmark of the new agriculture, driven by the expertise of Arab irrigators drawing on their long experience of oasis cultivation. Certainly, irrigation had been practised since antiquity in all the newly Islamic lands, but many of these systems were in terminal decline. Although few really innovative hydraulic technologies were invented at this time, the revival and expansion of irrigation through the widespread adoption and improvement of well-known devices and structures, including water-lifting machines, qanāts, diversion dams, distribution networks, siphons, and storage reservoirs, married to new Islamic institutions and legal frameworks for the equitable distribution and management of water, and the undoubted

Folio from an Arabic version of *De materia medica* by Dioscorides.
Written and illustrated by Abdullah ibn al-Fadl. Iraq, 1224
13.152.6 / Rogers Fund, 1913 / The Metropolitan Museum of Art

skill of the irrigators themselves, transformed the agricultural landscape.

The diffusion of new crops and cultivars, the adoption of new multiple-cropping and rotation regimes, the abundant use of manures, and the refinement and expansion of irrigation were supported, crucially, by changes in land tenure and taxation that accorded farmers more liberty and a greater incentive to improve their land, all underpinned by Islamic precepts and customary laws by which farming was conducted more fairly and more effectively. For the first time in many places, any individual – man or woman – had the right to own, buy, sell, mortgage, and inherit land, and, most importantly, farm it as he or she liked. Relatively low rates of taxation, where they existed at all, were paid as a fixed proportion of output, freeing farmers from uncertain and capricious tax hikes – in contrast to the oppressive rural taxation prevailing in the late Roman, Sassanian, and Byzantine empires. Large estates, which had everywhere come to dominate and often monopolise agriculture, were often broken down into smaller ownerships, or at least had to compete with smaller farms and individual peasant smallholdings. The lands around cities were almost everywhere given over to small market gardens and orchards. Serfdom and slavery were virtually absent from the countryside in the early Islamic world; instead, "the legal and actual condition of the overwhelming majority of those who worked on the land was one of freedom".

These are the salient features of the new agricultural system which has been called Moorish agriculture in relation to

Spain, but which is more properly and inclusively termed Islamic agriculture, for it was not confined to Moorish Andalusia; and although its origins lay in the intensive, irrigated, multi-storey, mixed-crop farming of the ancient Arabian oases and wadis, it was not exclusively Arab either, but developed in association with the traditional knowledge and skills of farmers right across the new Muslim world under the impetus and aegis of Islam.

We are printing this excerpt thanks to a generous agreement with the Filāḥa Texts Project. For more information, visit their website: filaha.org

ANO:
Mother Country

The collaboration and interactions afforded by the Venice Biennale have allowed Caravane Earth to expand our network of experts and friends. One such encounter led us to Nana Oforiatta Ayim, who was the curator of Ghana's first pavilion at the Venice Biennale in 2019. Her work as a cultural policy maker and curator very much resonates with the themes and plans of Caravane Earth. Here, she discusses the origins and critical phases of the organisation she founded – ANO Institute of Arts and Knowledge – and gives a glimpse of what is to come.

I started ANO twenty years ago next year, very young still but with the foresight of creating an umbrella term for the work I was then beginning. The term ANO came from the Akan word "εno", which means grandmother. It was a name my father used to call me when I was little, because he said I was sometimes wise like an old woman, but more than anything it summoned for me the old women that would come and sit on the porch of my mother's small house in Kyebi in the rainforests of Ghana, at the funerals or festivals that we went home for. They would tell me the origins of names, of families, of places. They would tell me the meanings of things. To me they felt like the keepers, the fount, of our cultural knowledge, and I wanted to sit in their midst forever and learn. It also came from the suffix in Esperanto, -ANO, that denotes belonging.

ANO's first foray was an exhibition of contemporary Ghanaian art for the Liverpool Biennial, the only African art exhibit present at the time. This was followed by more exhibitions, then films, all under the umbrella of ANO. I did not know at the time what I was building. What I did know was that I wanted to create something for people like me, a space in which we could come together, commune, exchange, learn, and be safe.

ANO found its way back home to Ghana in 2012 after stints in Ethiopia and Senegal, with the aim of setting up in the very house of my mother where I had learned so much. But by then my mother had passed away, and the male members of my family in Ghana did not understand what I wanted to create: a centre for our histories, our preservation, our reconnection. My dream of a centre in the mountains was deferred. And I began to lay foundations in the slightly more removed landscape of Accra.

It started out as an attempt to create a space within which I and people like me could belong, connect; to also explore the places we emerged from, where we stood, where we might be heading. I had left the "art worlds" that ANO and I had inhabited in the West for ten years because of their focus on materialistic exchange, and had found on arriving in Ghana a place where there was the struggle of no infrastructure, no safety nets, and no funding, but also the spirit of true experimentation and enquiry.

In its first five years in Ghana, ANO, by successfully attempting to bring about connections, greater resonance, and networks, but without the necessary discernment, managed to inadvertently and heartbreakingly help recreate the very mechanisms of commerce and profit over integrity left behind in Europe.

Now it is almost ten years since I've come home and ANO has been through so many iterations and inhabited so many roles. It started as a research hub, moved into artists' development, veered off into an art gallery, hosted workshops and talks, created leadership fellowships, built archives, advised governments, and took its exhibi-tions and workshops into marketplaces and squares across the country.

In all that time, ANO has kept asking itself, what is the right kind of structure for these contexts we inhabit? What institution grows out of the act of listening to all that is around?

Whilst attempting to find a way out of the narrow cultural confines of the white cube space – the "universal" museum – ANO began to look at structures and forms that seemed accessible to all, grounded in the vernacular of exchange across the country. It found two models: the kiosk and the "Afahye", or festival. I created a mobile museum that travelled across the country and into communities, and through this journeying found the kind of connections that I had been searching for, in particular in the realms of indigenous knowledge systems and the wisdom and pragmatism encapsulated within them. They had been passed down, grown, and developed over thousands and thousands of years. They encompassed the arts and education, as well as science and technology, psychology, mythology, and cosmic knowledge. They were an integrated system in which the human was only a small part of a much greater whole. What I had been looking for was not dying, had not been destroyed by colonialism, but was literally there, waiting to be drawn upon.

ANO was birthed by the stories of mothers and grandmothers, by the personal and collective need for belonging. And so coming up to its twentieth year, it began to come back full circle to a dream of belonging to oneself, the earth, to the rhythms of being birthed of centuries of becoming. I always had a dream of life lived in harmony with nature, of growing one's own food, of creating a school grounded within our shared knowledge, in which children grow in freedom; in which art and culture are but one strand of a larger ecology of being.

Last year, as Covid took hold of the world and all was shocked into stillness, this dream of growing our own food began to take shape concretely, on a piece of land I had bought in Aburi, just outside of Accra. The dream of a school began to be manifested, in collaboration with a neighbour of the land who shared that dream. In Accra, the dream of a space where people could come from all over the continent of Africa and beyond to give form to how their creations, thoughts, and trajectories of indigenous knowledge systems might flow into the present, is being solidified in a raffia palm structure. I am beginning to create structures that draw on our indigenous knowledge systems bolstered by research collected through ANO's Pan-African Cultural Encyclopaedia, and then investigate what holistic, conscious learning and cultural exchange mechanisms might look like in our context, both for children and adults.

For this, I am drawing on new aligned networks formed across the still so-called Global South rather than across the North-South divide; on new paradigms and frameworks like pluriversalism, post-developmentalism, degrowth, and buena vida, especially in places like Latin America, where there is a convergence of movements for social justice, ecology, and indigenous peoples; and in educational examples, like the Green School that began in Bali.

Local sustainable materials that house us. Ways of growing, healing, and nourishing that we have learnt over centuries. Ways of learning to be in the world, in harmony with it, that have been passed down despite the many attempts at rupture.

Creatures of the
Soil, Reborn

Tim Ingold, Chair of Social Anthropology at the
University of Aberdeen and author of numerous
publications, works with a wide range of issues, from
art and architecture to ecology, theories of evolution,
and human-animal relations. He looks at the origins
of the word "human" and the affinity of humans
with soil, particularly in its capacity for renewal and
regeneration.

"Human" is an ancient word. It's been around for a very long time. But the concept of humanity is a modern invention. No one knows exactly where the word "human" comes from, but Giambattista Vico, in his *New Science* of 1725, thought the source of the word lay in the Latin word for burying – humando – which itself comes from humus, meaning soil. So humans would above all be people of the soil, who bury their dead. They come from the earth, and will ever return to it. However, thinkers of the Enlightenment, among them Vico himself, would eventually upend this logic, appealing instead to universal powers of reason or intellect, destined to emancipate humankind from earthly bondage and to cut all ties to the ground, to place, and to nature. The modern concept of humanity has its source in this inversion, in the establishment of what we often call the "human condition", over and above the state of nature that is supposed to hold other creatures in its grip. And nature, by the same token, was no longer deemed to be enriched and fortified by the labours of generations past; it was treated rather as both a platform for human endeavours and a depository for a history whose energy is spent, leaving its residues piled up in layers of sediment, each covering over its now submerged predecessors.

Thenceforth, the ground – understood as a passive substrate, rather than an active and energising force in the ongoing generation of life – could be excavated with impunity. Digging up the past, once associated with the dark arts of necromancy, became a respectable antiquarian profession. And with

that, archaeology was born, along with the idea of the human career as an ascent from brute nature through shades of savagery and barbarism to the perfection of the human condition in refined civility. Of this career only the later phases, initiated by the onset of written records, were considered to be truly historic. Everything prior to this watershed was considered preparatory for civilisation, much as childhood was considered preparatory for adult life. Real history is for grown-ups. Thus, the very idea of a preparation for history, or what came to be known as "prehistory", was a direct precipitate of Enlightenment humanism. Yet many contemporary scholars proclaim the days of humanism to be over, or at least numbered.

<blockquote>
We are entering –
they say – a new era,
that of post-humanity.
So what will become of
the idea of pre-history
then?
</blockquote>

There can be no doubt that humanism has contributed massively to the common good. It has brought education, literacy, and democratic governance to more of the world's inhabitants than ever before. And commensurate with this success, what began in a handful of European nations has expanded globally through trade and colonisation. But this has come at a cost in two respects. First, in driving a wedge between humanity and nature, the very earth that had once offered nourishment and support for human life came to be recast as a repository of resources to be plundered. Archaeological excavation thus figured as a mere prelude to a programme of extraction on an industrial scale, that has ravaged the earth and jeopardised its capacity for renewal. And second, while the appeal to universal entitlement serves the interests of those empowered to lay claim to it, for others the forcible imposition of this claim has meant enslavement, along with loss of land, livelihood and even life. In the history of colonialism, the flag of humanity has always been flown by the victorious, treating as less than human those who have come under its yoke. As these twin costs have inexorably risen, what began as an agenda for progressive emancipation has morphed into a vicious spiral of environmental destruction and social injustice. To break the spiral demands no less than a radical alternative to the humanist settlement. For scholars, the challenge is to create a language of concepts in which to frame it. This is the challenge of post-humanism. The question I want to pose is this: what role will the ground, the soil, or the earth play in a future post-humanist settlement?

II

Let me begin by going back to Vico's speculation that humans, at least in the etymological sense of the term, are distinguished above all by their affinity to the soil, revealed in the habit of burying their dead. Whether or not Vico's etymology is well-founded – and most scholars are convinced that it is not – it is sufficient to acknowledge that the word "human" is indeed very old and that it tells us something about humans in relation to the soil and to burial. For many humans do bury their dead, and these burials have yielded rich pickings for prehistorians and archaeologists. But the burial of the past is quite different from the deposition of the past.

Burial is part of a cycle of life that carries on over generations; in it lies the potential of generations past to produce those to come.

Rather like a seed or a tuber that the farmer plants in the hope that it will take root and grow, the human body in burial harbours in itself the forces of renewal that will bring forth future life. But excavation, as practised by archaeologists, breaks the cycle by extracting the body from the ground rather than allowing it to regenerate.

That's why excavation has proved so contentious, above all in the campaigns waged by archaeologists, in the wake of colonisation, to unearth the pasts of peoples native to colonised lands. For archaeologists immured in the idea of history as the positive impulse of human progress, the grave was a kind of double negative, wherein the dead, already deposited below ground in bygone times, were doubly submerged as the grounds of antiquity themselves sank beneath subsequent layers of historical sediment. The burial ground, far from providing a foundation for progressive humanisation, as Vico saw it, would come to be regarded as a site of dehumanisation, of the dissolution and decay of humanity into nature. That's why archaeologists saw nothing wrong in emptying the graves they discovered of their bones and artefacts, and in transporting them to faraway museums for analysis and display.

To disinter the burial, to dig it up, is to render this guarantee null and void. Whether the damage can ever be repaired by repatriating the remains is moot. The cycle of life once broken is not easily made whole again.

III

Everything depends here on how we imagine the ground. What kind of surface is it? Can you roll it up – as you can a carpet or a sheet of paper – into a scroll? If you want to buy turf to restore your lawn, you can go to a garden centre and buy a roll of grass with a thin layer of soil underneath. But it is not otherwise possible to roll up the ground. It is, however, possible to turn it. Consider the medieval ploughman who would turn the ground with every seasonal turn in the agricultural calendar: in April for spring crops, in June for the late summer harvest, and in October for winter wheat and rye. The purpose of ploughing was both to prepare the earth for future planting by breaking up the surface residues of the previous crop, and to bring up nutrient-rich soil from deeper down. Thanks to this continual turnover, the ground will continue to yield year after year. Following a cycle of rotation, fertility born of the past bears fruit in present flourishing.

Indeed, the ground, speaking to the husbandman with the bounty of previous harvests, was a surface not just of cultivation but of remembering. With every turn, memories of persons who lived or events that happened long ago would be brought to the surface so that inhabitants could engage with them directly, as if they were present in the here and now. This precisely parallels how the pages of a book were read in medieval times. It was supposed that the page would speak to the reader with the voices of the past – its letters and words springing to life in the present just like seeds germinating in the soil. With the page as with the ground, the past would rise up even as the present sinks down, and time, as it passed, would continue to turn.

In the modern imagination, however, enshrined in the political logic of the territorial state, the ground is not for turning. It is for conquest, colonisation, and occupation. The state – far from inscribing its ways as does the husbandman into the land, or the penman into parchment – imposes sovereignty from above, very much as with the printing press, letters are imposed from above upon the sheet. Just as every new impression calls for a new sheet, so every inscription in the land calls for a new ground. The ground figures here not as a surface to be actively restored and cultivated, but as a passive substrate upon which to map out the strategic designs of the present. As such, it holds no potential for renewal. For the past is already over, sunk into its own stratum, overlain in the execution of present designs. And whatever their claims to perpetuity, these designs are destined to be covered over in their turn by those of the future.

Renewal depends not on turning but on superimposition – on adding another layer to the stack, and then another, and another.

The earth's depth is now understood to be not so much enrolled in a cycle as layered in a stack, wherein every layer belongs to its own time, only to be superseded by the next.

Time, then, no longer turns the ground into a volume, like a scroll. It rather pierces through successive grounds like an arrow, pointing either upwards from past to present, or downwards from present to past. Every ground, every layer, establishes its own plane of synchrony, while layer succeeds layer in a diachronic sequence. Herein lies the source of the opposition between synchrony and diachrony, which has proved so fundamental to modern thought. The implication is that to reach the past, as in an archaeological excavation, you have to dig down. With this, memory is deposited like papers in an archive, so as to form a stack. The older the record, the further down it lies. And there it stays, sinking ever deeper as time moves on.

IV

If you have managed to follow my argument so far, you will see that whether we're speaking of the page or the ground, we end up with a distinction between two kinds of surface. One is a layered surface which covers up what went before and is closed to what follows. The other is a deep surface that covers nothing but itself and yet rises into the open.

I have presented these as alternatives, even to the extent of aligning them to a contrast between modernity and tradition. And yet this contrast is surely artificial. Perhaps it's more reasonable to suppose that these alternative understandings of the ground surface, far from standing on opposite sides of a great divide in the history of the world, have always coexisted and have continually answered to one another. In different periods or regions, one side may have been ascendant or given greater ideological prominence, but the other would have always been present in the background. It is, after all, in the nature of ideologies to be lopsided, and they can deceive by leading us to mistake one kind of surface for another. This, incidentally, is how camouflage works. It tricks the perceiver into supposing that what is actually a double-sided layer covering up that which is hidden within or beneath is really a face that is open to the world. So the military commander paints the tarpaulins under which he conceals his tanks in motley shades of green and brown, rendering them indistinguishable to aerial reconnaissance from the face of the earth. But the face of the earth – just like the face of a human being – is a front without a back. And having no back, it appears to have nothing to hide.

But the deceit can work the other way as well, though perhaps less intentionally. In many parts of the world, landscapes are dotted with mounds of various sizes, from the insignificant to the monumental. They've been around since time immemorial; prehistorians call them tumuli, or mounds. Just how and why tumuli were formed remains a matter of controversy which need not detain us here. Suffice it to note that any accumulation of waste material, whether from the construction of earthworks or from everyday domestic habitation, is liable to settle more or less of its own accord into the form of a mound. If you are on the beach at the seaside, and digging a hole in the sand for fun, the sand you have already dug and put to one side will form a mound more or less of its own accord. As such, the mound is nothing more than a swelling of the earth that covers nothing and is open to the elements. But this has not deterred legions of prehistorians from excavating their tumuli in the conviction that buried inside each must be a body. There must be something inside, something underneath we should excavate. Occasionally they have struck lucky and been rewarded with sensational finds. But more often than not, their excavations have yielded only quantities of earth and rubble. Their error has been to imagine the face of the earth as a twin-sided layer or enclosure which, consequently, must have something to hide. But could the practice of burial point to a different conclusion?

V

Let's go back to Vico and his ideas about the human as a creature that buries its dead. Might burial establish a peculiarly human relation to the ground and to the past, in which opening and closure, far from being mutually exclusive, may actually alternate? Let's imagine the phases of the burial as it might have been practised in antiquity. First the earth is opened. Material is removed to form a pit, into which the body is laid (incidentally, as the pit is dug, a mound of earth will form on one side). Following the necessary ritual formalities, the pit is then covered with a slab of stone. In the grave, this slab forms a layer with two sides – upper and lower, concealing the body beneath. But for the living, sealing the slab does nothing to extinguish the memory of the deceased. On the contrary, it remains deeply engraved in their hearts and minds. Yet with the passage of time and generations, memories gradually fade, even as vegetation encroaches over the slab, contributing through its decomposition to the formation of soil. Eventually, after many centuries or even millennia, the grave site is left indistinguishable from its surroundings, save perhaps for a small hump or a stone to mark its location. Once again, the ground of the site shows its face to the sky. With the grave long forgotten, people go about their lives completely unaware that anything lies below, until, perhaps, it is exposed by natural erosion or the ministrations of archaeologists.

As this story of burial shows, bringing closure to the past is one thing, wiping it out altogether is quite another.

Just as the insomniac's attempts to fall asleep make him all the more wakeful, so our efforts to forget the past have the opposite effect of bringing it more vividly to mind. Yet as surely as sleep eventually comes, so the past will be forgotten. In the mind, however, as in the landscape, it fades not by sinking deeper down, but by rising to the surface, only to be wiped away by the elements.

Drawing a line over the past or sealing it underground will not make it go away.

What does all this mean for the way we think about memory? I have shown that our modern sensibilities are profoundly conditioned by the idea that everything is formed of layers – that the ground, trees, buildings, books, and even human minds are built up layer upon layer with each layer already marked up with its own striations. The past, then, is visible only by way of the translucence of the present. We have to be able to see through the present to see the past. But the ground as a surface teaches us otherwise. It tells us that with the passage of time, material is not added but worn away through erosion, and that to mark it up means cutting deep. Our oldest memories, then, are not the deepest, nor are the most recent memories the shallowest. On the contrary, what is furthest in the past is closest to the surface. Both in our minds as well as in the ground we tread, our recent deeds and words are most profoundly seared,

while traces of the distant past are so shallow as to be on the point of disappearing altogether, erased by the winds of present suffering. Like old paths grown so faint as to be no longer recognisable, mcmories only truly fade as they surface into our present, the texture of which – rather like the texture of a veil – is opaque.

There is surely a lesson here for tyrants everywhere who believe that their murderous acts can be struck out, deleted from the record and hidden underground. They imagine the ground as a cover-up, thinking that beneath it, the evidence can be forever concealed from posterity. This is literally to overlook the past in both senses of the word. It is to keep it under surveillance, but at the same time to turn a blind eye. Yet deeds will have their comeuppance, and will only be gone once and for all when they finally surface to be wiped out by the ravages of time. Perhaps, then, the ground, the soil, offers a milieu not just for burying the past, but for future renewal.

ADDITIONAL CAPTIONS

L'Abbazia di San Giorgio Maggiore
Page 16
Giorgio Sommer, c. 1860–90
RP-F-F01182-X / Rijksmuseum
Pages 18–19
Carlo Ponti, 1860–1870
84.XM.501.8 / J. Paul Getty Museum
Pages 20–23
Author unknown, c. 1860–80
3320-1920, E.94-2019, 3320-1920, E.57-2019 / Victoria
and Albert Museum

The Majlis: Curatorial Narrative
Pages 34–35
A View of the Majlis Exhibition

Artefacts from the Majlis Exhibition
Page 37
Carpet. The majlis of Shirin and Khosrow
Kashan, Iran, first half of the 20th century
FBQ. 7394 / Sheikh Faisal Bin Qassim Al Thani Museum
Page 38
The San Rocco Mamluk carpet

A Collection of Stories without Borders
Page 57
Bird-Shaped Incense pot
Iran, 13th century
FBQ. 2037 / Sheikh Faisal Bin Qassim Al Thani Museum
Pages 62–63
Jar (Tear Collector)
Iran, 17th century
FBQ.44 / Sheikh Faisal Bin Qassim Al Thani Museum
Pages 66–67
Vase
Syria, 20th century
FBQ. 2038.1_2 / Sheikh Faisal Bin Qassim Al Thani
Museum

King Fuad's Khayamiya Textiles in a Dutch Museum
Page 73
Set of khayamiya textiles on display in the Majlis
exhibition, Venice, in 2021, c. 1933, Egypt.
Dutch National Museum of World Cultures, long term
loan from the Oosters Institute. Photograph by Simone
Padovani

Jörg Gruber on Documenting Craft
Pages 86–87
M'hammad the shepherd and his family
Near Ain Leuh, Atlas Mountains, Morocco, 2019
Pages 90–91
Bamboo plantation El Quindío Colombia, 2019

The Path of Bamboo with Simón Vélez and Stefana Simic
Pages 100, 104–105, 108–109, 112–113, 116–117
Photographed in Manizales (Colombia) during the
prototyping process of the Majlis, 2019

Documenting Architectural Tradition
Page 121
Al-Sulaiman Palace, Jeddah, Saudi Arabia, 1979

A Network For Preserving Tradition
Page 131
Engelsberg Summer School in Classical Architecture,
Germany

Creating Spaces for Islamic Art
Page 139
Grand Musée de Marrakech, Marrakech, Morocco

The Atlas Weavers
Pages 144, 146–150
Photographed during a Caravane Earth team field trip to
Morocco in 2019

Making Artisan Voices Heard
Page 152
Ain Leuh Women's Weaving Cooperative
Atlas Mountains, Morocco, 2019

Living with the Art of Craft
Page 175
The Earl of Snowdon, known in the world of furniture as
David Linley
Photo © LINLEY furniture

The Multifaceted World of Craft
Page 178
Passamaquoddy basket maker Molly Neptune Parker
of Princeton, Maine, was a revered tribal elder and the
longtime president of the Maine Indian Basketmakers
Alliance
Photo by Tom Pich Photography/NYC

An Introductory Survey of Arabic Books and Farming
Almanacs of Filāḥa
Page 215
Folio from an Arabic translation of the *De materia
medica* by Dioscorides. Written and illustrated by
Abdullah ibn al-Fadl. Iraq, 1224
1977.91 / John L. Severance Fund / The Cleveland
Museum of Art

ACKNOWLEDGEMENTS
WE THANK THE FOLLOWING
FOR THEIR ADVICE AND SUPPORT:

Professor Abdel-Wahed El Wakil
Professor Salma Samar Damluji
Mohammed Al Attiya
His Excellency Nasser Al Hinzab
Dr Yousef AlHorr
Hassan Al Mulla
Fatma Al-Remaihi
Sheikha Amna Al Thani
Feras Al Yasin
His Excellency Youssef Balla
Salouha Bentaher
Toto Bergamo Rossi
Dr Alexandra Bounia
Prof.ssa M.Agnese Chiari Moretto Wiel
Claudio Cravero
Arch. Barbara Foscari
Professor Deborah Howard
Dr Marjorie Hunt
Dr Sarah Johnson
P. Hamazasp Kechichian
SABAP per Venezia e Laguna
Dr Richard Kurin
Christelle Le Déan
Dr Patrick Linke
Dr Karim Lahham
Professor Wayne Modest
Avv. Giacomo Montanari
Princess Nina Lobanov-Rostovsky
Avv. Teresa Lo Torto Alessandri
Olivier Morel DPLG
Prof. Alberto Peratoner
Professor Mikhail Piotrovsky
Dr Nestor Ponguta
Arch. Franco Posocco
Her Excellency Gloria Isabel Ramirez Rios Matteo
Rosati
Richard Taylor
Ana Luiza Thompson-Flores
Harriet Wennberg
Magnus von Wistinghausen
Boghos Arciv. Levon Zekiyan

PUBLIC RELATIONS
CONSULTANTS

Bolton & Quinn

ART HANDLING AND
TRANSPORTATION

Interlinea Srl
Barbara De Zorzi
Claudio Zambon
Renzo Busetto

INSTALLATION

Architect and Engineer
Arch. Bruno Ranuffi
Ing. Davide Beltrame
Majlis Textile Installation
BIBIBAFT
Mohsen Chavoshbaran
Mostafa Charkhandaz
Kamran Ajal

ABBAZIA DI SAN GIORGIO
MAGGIORE TEAM

Abate Emerito Norberto Villa o.s.b.
Dom Giacomo Pedron o.s.b.
Ingrid Fournival
Mario Volpato
Fiorello Pellizzari
Paola Elena Florea
Alessandro Colombo

ABBAZIA DI SAN
GIORGIO MAGGIORE

Abate Stefano Visintin o.s.b.
Carmelo Grasso Direttore Benedicti Claustra Onlus

EXHIBITION LOANS

Sheikh Faisal Bin Qassim Al Thani Museum
The Dutch National Museum of World Cultures
Monastero di San Lazzaro degli Armeni
Scuola Grande di San Rocco
Dott. Taher Sabahi
Mohsen Chavoshbaran

CARAVANE EARTH TEAM

Managing Director:
Fahad bin Mohammed Al-Attiyah

Deputy Managing Director:
Rajae El Mouhandiz

Operational Director:
Suriya Ali

Director of Communications:
Furqat Palvan-Zade

Art Director:
Igor Garin

Project Managers:
Anneloes Bakker
Rasima Isaeva

Curator & Community
Engagement:
Farah Al Yasin

Creative Programming:
Galya Bott

Infrastructure & Sustainability:
Johann Bott

THE MAJLIS TEAM

Curator:
Dr Thierry Morel

Architects:
Simón Vélez
Stefana Simic

Landscape Design:
Todd Longstaffe-Gowan
Clay Baylor
Abhi Ramachandra

Partnerships and Symposia:
Johnny Cornwell

Photography:
Jörg Gruber

Colombia Craftsman Team:
Alonso Cardenas
Fernando Osorio
Jose Nixon Ocampo
Jose Anibal Ochoa
Jorman Silva

Gigagrass Team:
Raquel Ganitsky White
Diana Barrera Salazar

Majlis Roof and Wall Textiles:
Omar Zaidani
Mehdi Benelmah

Ain Leuh Weavers:
Hachmia El Douiri
Khadouj Ouchkek
Khadija El Aabdi
Fatima Abaraou
Hjoui Amrani

Tent Roof and Wall
Weaving Team:
Ahmed Chmiti
Fatima Chmiti Atti

Artist:
Irini Gonou

Textiles and Interiors:
Prerna Saraff
Nina Mohammad-Galbert

Conservation Consultants:
Helen Glanville
Paolo Roma —
MAUVE srl, Venice

Line Producer:
Heather Doole

Project Manager Venice:
Leif-Erik Hannikainen

Horticultural Advisers:
Mark Straver
Hortus Loci
Dott.ssa Isabella Dalla Ragione

CATALOGUE TEAM

Editors:
Furqat Palvan-Zade
Ben Wheeler
Lesia Prokopenko

Design:
Timur Akhmetov
Sasha Kulikov

Photo Editor:
Nastya Indrikova

Publisher:
Fontanka
5A Bloomsbury Square
London WC1A 2TA

ISBN: 978-1-906257-37-8

PARTNERS

Bolton & Quinn

OFFICIAL AIRLINE
SPONSOR

Published by Caravane Earth for the
2021 Venice Architecture Biennale.

This book is the result of collective work by the teams of
the Caravane Earth foundation and the Majlis project. We
would like to express our sincere thanks to our network of
collaborators, experts, and partners for their participation
in this publication.